Recollections of a Private of the 68th (Durham) Regiment of Foot

Recollections of a Private of the 68th (Durham) Regiment of Foot

During the Walcheren Expedition and the Peninsular War, 1806–15

ILLUSTRATED

John Green

LEONAUR

Recollections of a Private of the 68th (Durham) Regiment of Foot
During the Walcheren Expedition and the Peninsular War, 1806-15
by John Green

ILLUSTRATED

FIRST EDITION IN THIS FORM

First published under the title
The Vicissitudes of a Soldier's Life: Or a Series of Occurrences from 1806 to 1815

Leonaur is an imprint of Oakpast Ltd
Copyright in this form © 2023 Oakpast Ltd

ISBN: 978-1-916535-36-7 (hardcover)
ISBN: 978-1-916535-37-4 (softcover)

http://www.leonaur.com

Publisher's Notes

The views expressed in this book are not necessarily
those of the publisher.

Contents

Preface

The outlines of the following sheets were drawn up several years ago, solely for my own amusement, not in the least anticipating their appearance before the public eye. I made notes of several of the particulars contained in this *Narrative* when I was in the Peninsula, especially while at Freynada; the greater part, however, were written immediately after my return to England. In this state they continued until the year 1825, when, having much leisure time, I thoroughly revised the whole of what I had previously written, and gave it what I conceived to be a more connected form of arrangement, beginning with my departure from home, and ending with my return to Louth subsequent to my discharge.

After I had written about one hundred folio pages, I showed them to some of my friends, who strongly advised me to publish my *Narrative*, promising me very liberal support. Induced by these persuasions, I at length consented, and began to prepare for presenting to the public my little work.

That the *Narrative* may be more acceptable to readers in general, I have divided the whole into chapters, and also given an introductory and a concluding chapter, which will introduce before the reader the rise and termination of the Peninsular War.

My own *Narrative* will give the intermediate part. I have confined myself principally to facts which for the most part came under my own immediate notice; for those which did not, especially in the introductory and concluding chapters, I am indebted to Baines's *History of the War*, and Gifford's *Life of Wellington*.

I now present my performance to the candour of the public, and beg leave to apologise for thus intruding myself upon their notice. I make no lofty pretensions: I make no boast of having undergone more than other men, or of having performed anything extraordinary; nor have I attempted to put forth anything in the shape of elegant composition: I have simply endeavoured faithfully to give a plain unvarnished tale; and as no account of this nature—*viz.* as to what generally happens to a common soldier in serving during a series of campaigns—has as yet appeared in this part of the country; moreover, as I conceive that anything connected with the Peninsular War must be interesting to every Briton; I respectfully hope that this little production will not be altogether unacceptable to my readers.

J. Green

May 1827.

Introduction

Vast and important were the events which ultimately led to the breaking out of the Peninsular War. These events had their origin in the French revolution, the causes of which were visions and palpable. Among these may be reckoned the writings of the French philosophers; the intolerance and cupidity of the Romish clergy; the oppressed and degraded condition of the people; the liberties and prosperity of England; and, in particular, the republican principles imported from America by La Fayette and his followers. These and other circumstances conspired to produce one of the most tremendous and terrible revolutions ever recorded in the pages of history, which in its consequences set all Europe in a flame, and involved it in a war that raged for many years with great fierceness and animosity.

It was during this war that the celebrated Napoleon Buonaparte found his way to power; and so great was the influence he gained, and the terror he inspired, that all Europe, Great Britain excepted, trembled at his nod, and bowed beneath his feet. The success of the French arms under his direction, and his rapid elevation, were truly astonishing. In the course of ten years from the commencement of his career, (in which period he had obtained the title of First Consul, and afterwards those of Emperor of France, King of Italy, Protector of the Confederation of the Rhine, with many others,) his power seemed almost unlimited. The only effectual stand against him was made by Great Britain. She continually goaded him; opposed and marred his ambitious views; and in the end accomplished his ruin.

The north of Europe being secured by the treaty of Tilsit, and Buonaparte having no other object on the Continent worth his notice, directed his attention to Spain and Portugal. The existence of the Bourbons on the throne of Spain occasioned him much disquietude, and he thought, now was the time for deposing them, and placing the crown on the head of one of his own family. To effect this purpose, he took care to procure the admission of thirty thousand men under

Junot through Spain, for the invasion of Portugal, as well as of numerous other bodies within the Spanish territories, under the specious pretence of keeping off the incursions of the English, and of reducing Gibraltar.

Having obtained a footing, he artfully allured the royal family of Spain to Bayonne; where he forced the imbecile king to abdicate, and the Prince of Asturias to renounce all pretensions to the crown of Spain. He afterwards sent them into confinement; and dispatched his brother Joseph Buonaparte on the 8th of July 1808, with a splendid retinue, to take possession of the vacant throne. The Spaniards, perceiving their own folly at being duped, and exasperated at the perfidious conduct of the French, flew to arms with the greatest alacrity.

The first affair of any magnitude that took place between the contending parties, was at Baylen, in Andalusia, on the 20th of July, 1808. Murat, who was stationed at Madrid, had dispatched General Dupont with a body of troops to seize upon Cadiz. This general had scarcely passed the Sierra Morena, when he found himself opposed by General Castanos at the head of a large army of Spaniards. A battle ensued; the French were defeated, and most of their army taken prisoners: Cadiz was by this fortunate result preserved. Buonaparte was so incensed at this failure, that he forthwith ordered Dupont to be shot; Joseph Buonaparte, not deeming himself very safe at Madrid after this defeat, quitted it on the 1st of August, taking along with him a large booty, obtained by devastation and pillage.

The Portuguese in the meantime had begun to bestir themselves; and a *junta* having been formed at Oporto, they had applied to England for assistance. Accordingly, a body of nine thousand men had sailed from Cork in Ireland, on the 12th of July 1808, to assist the patriots. This body landed on the 1st of August, in Mondego Bay, in Portugal where they were joined by succours under Generals Spencer, Ackland, and Moore, the whole amounting to about thirty thousand men. The command of this force was entrusted to Sir Arthur Wellesley, the present Duke of Wellington.

Sir Arthur had no sooner landed, than he began to exhibit those abilities and powers of mind, which afterwards rendered him so illustrious and renowned in the annals of modern warfare. Having made all necessary preparations, he set out from Oporto on the 13th of August, defeated General Laborde on the 17th at Roleia, and on the 20th met Junot, who had set out from Lisbon with his whole force to oppose him. A pitched battle was fought at Vimiera between the hostile armies. In this battle the French received an early lesson, as to what kind of a reception they were likely to meet with from the English. Buonaparte's peculiar tactics, which on all other occasions had secured the victory, were here tried in vain.

The British soldiers took to their bayonets, with which they are aways irresistible, and the enemy fled. Although very superior in artillery and cavalry to the English, they were routed with the loss of four thousand men, besides twenty-one pieces of cannon, and stores of various kinds: while the total loss of the English in killed, wounded, and missing, only accounted to seven hundred and twenty, After this victory, Portugal was cleared of the enemy: Sir Arthur's presence was required in England, and the command of the army devolved upon Sir John Moore.

The Spaniards having solicited the aid of the English. Sir John Moore was ordered to proceed to Spain, marching in the direction of Burgos. He set out from Lisbon on the 31st of October. On his arrival at Sahagun, whither he had been led by the most flattering assurances of the Spaniards, he found the Spanish affairs in the most deplorable condition. All their armies were disorganised and dispersed; and Buonaparte had arrived in person at Madrid with a new levy of one hundred and sixty thousand conscripts, to complete the subjugation of Spain. Sir John Moore discovering his critical situation, from the vicinity of so formidable an enemy, immediately commenced a retreat.

After having marched two hundred and fifty miles over a mountainous and barren country, in the depth of winter, destitute of supplies, and pursued by a superior force under Soult, the British Army arrived under the walls of Corunna, on the 11th of January, 1809. Here a battle was fought, in which Sir John Moore was killed. The worn-out Britons were victorious. By the 17th, the troops were all embarked on board of transports, and they sailed for England.

The Spanish Peninsula was now fast hastening to its fall, when fortunately, about this time, a diversion was made on the part of Austria; and Buonaparte left Madrid, on the 22nd of January, 1809, to attend to his affairs in Germany, leaving the cause of Spain to the guidance of his marshals. The hostile preparations of Austria induced the British Government to try the issue of another campaign. Sir Arthur Wellesley was again sent out, and arrived on the 22nd of April at Lisbon, where the joy at his arrival was beyond all bounds.

The British Army amounted at this time to about thirty-five thousand men. Sir Arthur on his landing was appointed Marshal-General of the Portuguese troops; and on his arrival at Coimbra, took the command of the Allied Army. On the 6th of May he reviewed his army, on the 7th set out for Oporto, to dislodge Soult, who had posted himself there. On the 12th the contest began, which ended in the defeat of the French. Soult retreated into Spain, and Sir Arthur returned to Lisbon to adopt measures for assisting the Spaniards.

Sir Arthur was some time delayed at Lisbon through the petty jealousies of the Spanish Juntas. A plan of operations having been at length agreed upon with the Spanish General Cuesta; he left Lisbon, and led his army into Spain. On the 27th and 28th of June, a desperate action was fought with Marshal Victor at Talavera de la Reyna; and notwithstanding the inactivity and cowardice of the Spaniards, Sir Arthur remained master of the field. In this action the enemy were in point of numbers almost three to one. The loss on both sides was very severe: the British loss was five thousand three hundred and sixty-seven in killed, wounded, and missing; that of the enemy above ten thousand. Twenty pieces of cannon were taken. Sir Arthur Wellesley was now created Lord Wellington.

Notwithstanding the victory gained at Talavera, Lord Wellington, by reason of the supineness and inactivity of the Spaniards, and because Soult, Ney, and Mortier were hastening by forced marches to relieve Victor, found it necessary to retreat; therefore, having eluded his adversaries by a rapid and masterly movement, he withdrew his army into Portugal, and extended it along the frontiers. Nearly every fortress in Spain now fell into the hands of the enemy; the Spanish Armies were broken and dissipated; and the French having nothing to resist them in Spain, assembled a formidable army under Massena, who had particularly requested to be sent against Lord Wellington, for the reduction of Portugal.

The campaign of 1810 opened with the taking of Ciudad Rodrigo, and Almeida, by the French. Lord Wellington not deeming it prudent under existing circumstances to risk a general battle, retreated by the way of Coimbra to Torres Vedras near Lisbon, (where he had previously taken care to have lines so fortified as to be rendered impregnable,) destroying everything likely to be of service to the enemy along his line of march. Massena followed in close pursuit, confident that the English were in full retreat to their ships.

On his arrival at Alentqueer, he found himself miserably mistaken; he perceived that he had been entirely outwitted, and that his army had been decoyed into a most perilous situation by the superior genius of the British commander. Disappointed and chagrined, he retired to Santarem; and soon after, his army having undergone the greatest privations, he fled into Spain, pursued by Lord Wellington.

By this time a considerable reinforcement had arrived from England; and Lord Wellington lost no time in pursuing his adversary. A battle was fought at Fuentes d'Onora on the 5th of May 1811, which completed the liberation of Portugal from the presence of the French. Massena was now recalled, and was succeeded in his command by Marshal Marmont. Almeida and Olivença were recaptured; Ciudad Rodrigo was blockaded, and Marshal Beresford was sent to lay siege to Badajoz. A strenuous effort was made by Soult to raise the siege: in consequence of this, an obstinate battle was fought on the 16th at Albuera, in which Soult was defeated.

The loss on both sides in this action was immense: that of the allies was eight thousand, and that of the enemy nine thousand men. On the 3rd of June, Marmont broke up from the Tormes, to form a junction with Soult. Lord Wellington offered them battle on the 17th, near Elvas: this they declined, and retired into Spain, leaving His Lordship to prosecute the siege of Badajoz unmolested. In this siege he was occupied, when the regiment to which I belonged arrived at Oronches and joined the army.

CHAPTER 1

In Time of War

I was born at Nottingham, on the 15th of June, 1790; but my parents were natives of Louth, in the county of Lincoln; to which place they returned when I was about six months old. My father died when I was four years of age. In 1803 I was put apprentice, by my grandfather, to Mr. Foggitt, overseer of Mr. A. Eve's carpet manufactory. In May 1806 I left Mr. Foggitt, at whose house I had had a very good home, but where I in vain tried to settle, having a disposition to wander, which left me no rest until it was gratified. I quitted Louth, not without regret, and, frequently looking back as I went along, arrived at length at a place on the Grimsby road whence I had the last sight of the noble spire of Louth church.

Here, for a moment, my feelings overcame me, and I was constrained to weep, thinking of the many dear objects which that sight brought to my recollection, and that I should never see it or them again. What, however, added to my grief, was, I had not acquainted my grandfather with my intention to leave Louth, and, as my friends afterwards informed me that he was very much grieved at my conduct, I suffered a great deal of uneasiness on that account.

On my arrival at Hull by dusk in the evening of the next day, I went in quest of lodgings at a public house, where I was told I was a runaway apprentice, and that they would not harbour me. This repulse had such an effect upon my mind, that I dared not enquire anywhere else, but wandered from one place to another till I found a new-built house, into which I crept for shelter, and laying all night in one of the cupboards, with my bundle for my pillow, slept soundly until daylight. About five o'clock I arose, and betook myself to the new dock, where I lounged about a great part of the mornings in hopes of getting employment on board some of the vessels.

At length my attention was drawn to a large hand-bill posted upon a wall, advertising for seventy men to man the *Anne* privateer, which mounted fourteen guns, commanded by Charles East Walkden. Inquiring where this ship lay, and being directed to the place, I stepped on board, and asked the captain whether he would employ me: he answered, yes; and therefore, I began immediately to pull the ropes, and assist in anything that was to be done, without bidding, being too pleased with my good luck. The sailors with whom I dined gave me great encouragement, saying that we should take some Dutch East-Indiamen, and all get rich together: but these prospects were not able to prevent my thoughts from going back now and then to the remembrance of the good home I had left, and of the resentment I had brought upon myself from my grandfather and other relations, by leaving my excellent situation.

After dinner we again got to our employ: there was sufficient work for all hands: some were painting, others bending the sails, and a few were taking water and provision on board. There was a boat suspended by tackles from the fore and main mast, and another boat on the deck: one of the men being ordered to let go a certain rope or tackle, he by mistake let go the one that held the former boat, which fell upon the back of the head of one of the prize-masters, forced his chin on the edge of the other boat, and deprived him instantaneously of life. The unfortunate man bled very profusely, the blood running out of the scoopers of the ship into the dock: after washing the blood from the deck, we covered him with a flag called the Union Jack, and laid him on the quarter deck, until an inquest sat on his body.

If I had at that time been in possession of a thousand worlds, I would have given them to have been at home with my old master Foggitt. My reflections on this terrible accident rendered me very uncomfortable in mind, and the thoughts of battles, sudden deaths, and murders, now rushing into my fancy, chilled the blood in my veins. As I was then a lad only fifteen years of age, no wonder my alarm should have been so great on the sudden and melancholy death of this officer, especially as I had, for ought I knew, to remain on board with him during the night, and no one else with me: but I was, in the evening, overjoyed to find that my apprehensions in this respect had been groundless.

Next day I met with my godfather, who had a son on board the *Anne*, of the name of William Poxon: he took me with him the second night, and from him I learnt where an uncle of mine lived, who, when I called upon him and made myself known to him, behaved with much civility to me. After remaining about three weeks with the *Anne* privateer, I left her for a few days, and should not have returned, had not my uncle embarked on board of the same vessel, which circumstance made me resolve to go with him, let the consequences be what they might. He was one of the prize-masters, and used to take the management of the ship in turn with the other officers.

On the 4th June we received a commission from government, acknowledging our vessel as a ship of war: for no private vessel can act as such, unless so commissioned; but, when in commission, private vessels are duly acknowledged by the government; so that all the prizes they take are lawful, and the government has its share of whatever prizes are taken by a privateer.

After this, we got out of the dock into Hull Roads, and having waited there two or three days for hands, without being able to get our complement, weighed anchor, and dropped down the Humber, and took our station opposite to Great Grimsby, where our captain went on shore in search of more hands, of which we still wanted twenty or thirty to man us completely, our present number consisting of only forty-three men and seven boys, which was not sufficient to work the ship and the guns at the same time. There are required, at least, seven men to a gun, and we had not quite four: but the captain returned to the ship with little or no success.

The next day we again weighed anchor, and set sail in quest of some rich East-Indiamen "belonging to the Dutch," who were coming north about from the East-Indies. As soon as we got out of the Humber, we steered full north, and kept that course till we reached Peterhead, a small sea-port in the north of Scotland. To this place we came about three o'clock in the morning, and loaded one of our six-pounders, and rammed the wadding well home, in order to make a loud report, which in a short period brought two or three boats from the shore filled with fish.

One of the boatmen coming on board to pilot us, we lay too till afternoon, and our captain went to Peterhead in order to prevail upon some of the sailors to join us, but in this he was disappointed, as it appeared that the good people of this place were not in the fighting humour. In the afternoon we sailed due north, keeping that course till the next evening, when we reached the Orkney Isles. This day the wind blew very fresh; next day it was a storm: the ship rolled very much; sometimes the yard-arms nearly touched the water, and several heavy seas broke in upon our forecastle.

To me, who had never been at sea before, the situation was awful: I could not help thinking that the ship would go down, and mentioning my fears to one of the lads who had been at sea once before, he said he thought the same, but that we must keep our thoughts to ourselves. The storm still increasing, I and the lad just mentioned were ordered aloft to send down the mizzen-top gallant yard. I felt reluctant, but was obliged to go, great as my terror was of falling into the sea. I begun to ascend the mast, and with some difficulty reached the mizzen-top; I tried to ascend the next stage, and arrived in safety at the cross trees. None but those who have experienced these things can imagine what I felt on this occasion I but I suppose these feelings are, more or less, known to all who, for the first time, engage in this sort of employ.

After a day or two, dangers and difficulties became familiar to me. I could go even to the extreme of the maintop-sail yard with as little dread, as if I were walking the deck in calm weather. The storm having abated, we arrived in safety at the Shetland Isles, and lay too opposite the port of Lerwick, the capital of this numerous group of islands, and received from the inhabitants butter, eggs, milk, worsted hose, night-caps, and a quantity of small sheep; for which articles they received in return old clothes, which they preferred to money. After we had got what quantity of butter, eggs, &c. we wanted, the next morning we left Lerwick, in order to cruise in those seas, and had not got many leagues, before we met the *Phoebe* frigate.

She hailed us, and then sent a lieutenant to board us, who called over the names of the ship's company. After he had done this, he ordered five of our men to take their hammocks and chests, and to go with him, which they were compelled to do, but it was a gross violation of all law and justice, in this fellow, to take away our men, especially as we were so short of our number.

We continued to cruise on this station for two or three days: on the third day we met with another frigate; the officer boarded us, and called all hands to the quarter-deck, and, after looking at each man, returned to his vessel, wishing us success in our undertakings. The next morning, we saw a strange sail a-head, sailing before the wind; a sure sign to us that all was not right. We made all the sail we possibly could, in order to overtake her. We had our royals and stunsails set, for it was a dead calm: in a few minutes more another sail was, discovered behind, making all the haste she could to overtake us. She fired several cannons for us to lay too, but, being in chase of the first mentioned vessel, we did not wish to lose time by doing so.

At length our suspicions were excited of this vessel, and when she got within musket-shot, several shots were fired from her, which crossed the decks, only just passing over our heads. It was now high time to prepare for action, which we did by clearing away the chests, and removing everything from the decks that seemed to be in the way: our hammocks were already fixed in the bulwarks or sides of our vessel; all the cutlasses, muskets, pistols, and boarding-pikes, were on deck, every man was at his station; every gun loaded with a double charge, one canister, and the other a round shot; all the matches were on deck ready lighted, we had also some bars of iron in the galley-fire for the bow guns, not having sufficient matches: and there was I stationed betwixt decks, in order to hand up the hot bars of iron, by no means liking my situation, and looking anxiously at the sides of the vessel, which I expected every moment to see bored by cannon-balls.

At last, most fortunately, the vessel came along side, the commander of which said, in French, "Haul down your stunsails, or I will fire into you." To which our captain answered, by his interpreter, "You will excuse me, sir; I am in chase of the vessel a-head, and have been for several hours." The commander then demanded from whence we came, and what was our name: after answering which question, we demanded of them the like information, and found she was a privateer from the Isle of Jersey, a sloop cutter, well manned, and mounted with sixteen guns. The commander and our captain now became very friendly, and joined in pursuit of the other vessel: the cutter sailed faster than we did, and came up with the other vessel about eight o'clock at night, and we got up about nine, after a chase of sixteen hours.

We manned our boats, with armed men from both vessels, who boarded the ship without resistance. Our officers having examined their papers, which were not satisfactory, we forthwith took the ship, and made off for the nearest port. She was a very large, ship, under Danish colours, and was homeward bound from the East-Indies: her cargo consisted of coffee, spices, and silk, with various other articles of the produce of India. We would have gone into the port of Leith, or any of the Scotch ports; but the wind was contrary, and continued so until we reached the mouth of the Humber, into which we sailed with our India prize, which was larger than both our vessels put together.

The guard ship at the mouth of the Humber boarded our prize to examine her, which they had no business to have done, for the Danish East-Indiaman was from a country subject to the plague, so that the guard ship was put under quarantine as well as our own vessels; but the prize was detained much longer than either the guard or ourselves, we being liberated on the third day.

While we lay in Hull Roads, various were the reports concerning us: some said our cook had lost a part of his foot in the engagement: it is true he had lost a part of his foot, but it was in Greenland several years before this: others said we had bars of gold throwing about the decks; but all these were idle tales.

We lay in Hull Roads about three or four weeks, expecting to put to sea every day; but the captain being ill of the gout, and our commission being within a few days of its termination, all hopes of our again putting to sea were given up. On a Sunday morning in the beginning of August we weighed anchor, and sailed into the new dock. We secured the *Anne* there, and all hands left her; except the apprentices, and not one of us got a single farthing, either for wages or prize-money, to this day; at least, I never heard of such a thing taking place.

I have now due to me from the owners of this vessel above three pounds wages; so that this wonderful was-to-be-something came to nothing: indeed, it was worse than nothings to spend our time, for nearly three months, without wages. I remained at Hull about fourteen days, and then returned to Louth, with a number of strange and wonderful things to tell my acquaintances and friends, concerning my adventures in the *Anne* privateer.

CHAPTER 2

Enlists in the 68th Regiment

Upon my return to Louth, I was well received by my master, who was a man remarkable for forgiving those that offended him. My grandfather also forgave me, and allowed me six weeks board and lodging under his roof, to afford me an opportunity of improving my circumstances, which, however, at the end of the six weeks, were in no better state than they had been before. In consequence of a reprimand from Mr. A. Eve, I determined not to work any longer at Louth, and went home, got my clothes, and set off for Leeds. Scarcely had I reached the village of Elkington, near Louth, when my heart misgave me, and instead of proceeding on that road, I crossed the country and arrived at my uncle's, at Horncastle, that night.

I slept at his house, and told him I was going to Leeds: my friends at this town said they were sure I should soon become a soldier, but I thought differently. The event will show how much better they knew the tendency of my restless disposition than I did myself. The day after I proceeded to Lincoln, passed through, and slept at a village only six miles from the city, situated on the east bank of the Trent. The next morning I set off for Gainsborough, reached it about noon, and when just beyond the bridge leading to Bawtry a chaise overtook me, and gave me a lift to that place, where I remained all night.

The following morning I started again: another chaise overtook me, and conveyed me nearly to Doncaster, through which town I passed, and refreshed myself at the Red House, about five miles beyond Doncaster. The Leeds coach coming up, I thought I would ride the remainder of my journey: the coachman took me up, and whispered in my ear the fare would be four shillings. "Very well," was the answer; but I really had only two shillings and three-pence in my possession.

When we arrived at Leeds, I gave the driver two shillings: he returned the compliment by a sharp cut with his whip, which was not, perhaps, unmerited, by the deception I had practised upon him. Off I started for Mr. Brumfet's carpet factory, and immediately got employment there: the next day I paid my footing, but when Mr. Brumfet himself saw me, he refused to retain me, saying I was an apprentice: it is true I was an apprentice, but my master and I had parted by mutual consent.

I succeeded, however, in obtaining employ under a Mr. Howard, who had a small carpet factory at the Nether Mills, known amongst the carpet weavers by the name of the Isle of Patmos. I lodged with a widow, a worthy woman, whose husband had been hanged for horse stealing, or something of the kind; and continued to work at Patmos for three weeks, but the materials being so extremely bad, I could earn but little wages, especially as I had been used to work upon good stuff at Mr. Eve's factory. One day, when very earnest for work, an accident happened to my winder's wheel I had to go a mile and a half, to a turner, to get it mended: proceeding up a street called Kirkgate, I overtook a soldier belonging to the Royal Train of Artillery, who looked at me steadfastly, and proposed the question, whether I would enlist? I answered, "No", when he said he would give me sixteen guineas bounty for seven years' service; but the answer still was No; for I had no inclination whatever to enlist.

But he still pressed the point, until I consented, when he gave me a shilling, and enlisted me to serve His Majesty George III. in the Royal Train of Artillery, but being too low in stature, he took me to the Colonel of the 68th Durham Regiment of Foot, just returned from the West-Indies, who directed him to ask the doctor whether he supposed I should grow any higher, my height being then only five feet one inch and a half. The doctor ordered me to undress, to ascertain if I were sound; and, having finished his examination, sent me out of the room into a passage to put on my clothes, in which condition people passing might see me; he then made his report to the colonel that I was fit for service. This took place on the 24th October 1806. I was then sent to the orderly room of the regiment, and remained there that night.

The next day I was before Mr. Justice Sheepshanks, to be sworn in the questions being put "Have you fits, or are you an Apprentice?" to which I answered, "No."

"Are you willing to go?" said the magistrate; "I know your master. Eve, very well; if you do not wish to go, I will set you free." This was very kind of the justice, but I declined his offer, being so strongly bent

George Ramsay, 9th Earl of Dalhousie, 7th Division

upon going for a soldier. He then tendered to me the oaths: I took them, and have kept, and hope to keep them; for I loved old England, and I am sure with good reason, as by experience I know there is no better country in the world.

I will here introduce an anecdote respecting this justice. A countryman having some business with him, thought it a strange thing to call him Sheepshanks; and wishing to be a little more polite, knocked at the door, and when the servant came, said, "Does Mr. Sheeplegs live here?" The servant said, "No, but Mr. Sheepshanks does;" which convinced the man that this was his proper name,

I received two pounds in part of my bounty, which was only eleven guineas instead of sixteen, having been sworn in for seven years and six months, if at the expiration of that time it should be a peace, or three years longer, if war should continue, and not for an unlimited period. My bounty was soon spent, although I was no drinker: I scarcely know how it went; but before one month had passed over not a shilling of it remained. I had taken care, however, to pay my lodgings: the poor old woman, with several others of her sex, wept over me, saying, I was some poor body's child.

"Oh!" said these kind-hearted women, "he will go abroad, and be killed."

I answered, "Nay; there will soon be a peace, and I shall then return home to enjoy myself."

One reason why the poor women felt so much, was on account of my youth; indeed, I was a very young soldier, being only sixteen years of age.

The 68th Regiment was raised in the county of Durham, in the middle of the last century, by General Lambton. In the year 1800 this regiment was filled up by volunteers from the Irish militia, who swelled its number to two thousand five hundred: it was then made into two battalions, and sent out to the West Indies; they had not, however, been long there, when sickness so reduced them, that the second battalion was broken up, and put into the firsts and in August 1806 they returned to England, not more than one hundred strong. They were at the taking of the island of St. Lucia, also at the suppressing of a mutiny in the 8th West India Regiment, on which occasion several men were killed on both sides; but the India regiment was disarmed, and several of the men executed.

The principal loss sustained by the 68th Regiment, during their stay in the West Indies, was by sickness: they were there five years and a half, and lost during that period about two thousand men: great numbers of the men brought on sickness, disease, and, in many cases, deaths by the immoderate use of new rum. The bad climate of the West Indies, much aggravated, no doubt, in its effects by the fatal use of spirits, is said to destroy more men than many of our active campaigns, together with hard fighting, in various parts of Europe: and this appears to be the case; for few regiments lose in proportion to this, two thousand in a little more than five years. The West Indies, therefore, is frequently called the grave of Englishmen, and in this instance the phrase will apply correctly.

The 68th Regiment went out to the West Indies two thousand five hundred strong: it may be asked, what became of the remaining five hundred, together with the recruits received from England? Several of them were sent home invalided, and were discharged: the rest, with the exception of those who had returned with the regiment, had volunteered into other regiments stationed in the West Indies, liberty being always given for that purpose; and the men who thus joined other corps received a bounty of three guineas.

We continued in Leeds till the 27th November, and then marched to a pretty little town called Ripon, about twenty-seven miles north of Leeds: at this place I learnt my exercise, in the bowling green on the north side of the minster. I was quartered at the sign of the Lamb and Flag, in Skelgate, and afterwards was changed to the sign of the Turk's Head, which was kept by a widow, called Ellen Steel. She was like a mother to me, and in return for her kindness; I used to help her to brew and tun, or anything of the kind.

Opposite to her house was a man of the name of Thekstone, who kept a school; and who was so kind as to teach me to read and, write. He certainly bestowed considerable attention and labour upon me, so that, through his kind instruction, from time to time, I made some little improvement in useful knowledge. I took great delight in this school. Mr. Thekstone was a regular visitor at my quarters, being fond of a little beer, though by no means what we call a sot.

While at Ripon, we received recruits every week: I was the first recruit that joined, the 68th Regiment after they left India, the second was a youth called Forbes. In May and June 1807, we began to increase. our numbers rapidly: in August a large draught from the Irish militia, and another from the Durham militia, joined us: after this, another draught from the Second West York, besides several recruits from many parts of England, Scotland, and Ireland: so that, at the end

24

of 1807, we began to look like a regiment, before this we were only like a company.

The reverend the Dean of Ripon made a present of a great number of prayer-books to our men: I received one, and carried it with me into Holland, Portugal, and Spain.

At this place, one of our Irish recruits, having indulged too freely in drink, lost the government of himself, and meeting one of the officers in the street, knocked him down, told him he was not fit to wear a sword, and ill-treated him very much. The man was confined and brought to a court-martial, and sentenced to receive one hundred and fifty lashes, at such time and place as the commanding officer should think fit. At length the day arrived when the sentence was to be put into execution: the regiment paraded in the market-place at the usual hour, and then marched to the race-course, formed a square; fixed the halberts, and thus prepared to inflict the punishment incurred by the prisoner, who at length arrived, escorted by a file of the guard.

The judgment of the court-martial was then read, which sentenced him to receive the number of lashes above stated. The commanding officer ordered the culprit to strip, and the latter reluctantly complied. All of a sudden, a shout of indignation broke forth from the inhabitants, who had followed by hundreds to see the punishment inflicted: yet notwithstanding the shouts of the populace, who were violent in the extreme, the sentence was carried into execution. This being the first time I witnessed anything of the kind, I felt very ill, turned sick, and had like to have fallen in the ranks: indeed, several of my comrades fainted away, and were carried out of the square to a distance.

Some of the women, who had followed, screamed and cried; others of them called the commanding officer every bad name they could invent: indeed, we were under the necessity of placing sentries round our regimental square, to keep off the crowds who had collected in such formidable numbers. The man himself was not silent, although his punishment was comparatively light to what I have seen since that period: his noise, together with that of the people, had the desired effect; for, after receiving fifty lashes, he was pardoned, and taken down from the halberts. As we marched home, the inhabitants pelted us with stones and other missiles, calling our officers some very unbecoming names: the people might mean well, but it is absolutely necessary to punish such conduct, or no man could live in the army or navy.

On the 3rd November 1807, the rout came for us to march on the 5th from this very delightful and pleasantly situated town to Doncaster. I often think of Ripon with pleasure. While in it, I visited Studley. Park and Fountains Abbey, most delightful and enchanting places. The minster, too, much pleased me: in short, I left Ripon with a heavy heart.

Early on the morning of the 5th November the drums beat, we fell in, and marched through Boroughbridge to Wetherby, the next day to Ferrybridge and Pontefract; and, on the 7th, reached Doncaster. Here we lay for several weeks during the depth of winter, and received men from the Scotch, Irish, and English militias, besides a number of recruits from different quarters. In February 1808, we left Doncaster, and marched through Ferrybridge, Tadcaster, and York, to Malton; at which latter place we remained about seven days, when three companies were sent to Pickering, to one of which I belonged.

This little town is pleasantly situated on the main road from York to Whitby. On the 15th March, however, we left Pickering and Malton, and marched to York, and continued there till July 14th. I was very fond of York: we used to parade twice a-day in the minster-yard, Sunday excepted. While at this city, we had a man called Murphy, who wanted to scheme his discharge by sham fits; but having a suspicion they were not real, a large bottle of the spirits of salts was applied to his nose, which made the poor fellow jump up in the greatest agony, and promise he would never sham any more: he then joined his company, and kept his promise.

We had another man who had deserted three times: he was tried by a court-martial, and sentenced to be punished: the regiment marched three times to the riding-school at the horse barracks, for the purpose of inflicting the punishment, and he, every time, fell into a fit, so that the punishment was delayed: but, the third time, notwithstanding his fits, they tied him up and began to flog him, which soon brought him to himself, and let us know that his fits were not real; had they been so, he probably would not have come to himself in so short a time. His punishment was well merited; for a man that is regardless of his oath and solemn promise to serve his country, is guilty of a real crime.

About three weeks before the half-yearly inspection, we began to prepare for it by going through our evolutions and manoeuvres in the large barrack-yard: towards the latter end of the time; in order that the regiment might learn to be steady, we fired with blank cartridge. A man called Malfrey, about five men from myself to the right, of Captain Gough's company, had loaded his piece five times, it missing every time. The sergeant in the rear told him he dare not fire it off, the man declared if it was full of devils he would: he did so in the next volley, and the consequence was dreadful; for his musket bursted into several pieces, carrying away a part of his hand, and wounding and burning several men who were near him, so that this part of our line was thrown into confusion. I saw a dog run away with one of his fingers.

The poor fellow was taken to the hospital at these barracks, and underwent amputation: one of the other men who had got wounded, made ten times the noise the man did who lost his hand. When the general came, Malfrey was recommended to the board, and got one shilling a-day pension. After this, there was a disturbance between a party of our officers and some women of the town.

The lord mayor and our colonel, who lived near to each other, came out to see what was the matter: the colonel presently received a blow on the head, and the lord-mayor was driven into his house: this disturbance took place in Coney-Street, near the Black Swan Inn, about eleven o'clock at night, and in two or three days afterwards we received orders to march to Doncaster, in consequence of this shameful riot.

We arrived at Doncaster about the 18th July: on the 30th I went on command with two deserters to Stilton barracks, and had only just returned, when we received a route for Hull, where we arrived on, or about the 16th August, and were quartered the ropery-barracks in Wincolmlee. At Hull our duty was very hard, having to mount guard three times in the week. The whole of the troops used to parade every morning in George-Street, at eleven o'clock: those who mounted the main garrison, and South-End guards had to undergo the severe inspection of the brigade-major, who was a constant plague and torment to the soldiers: he has been known to reject the cleanest man in our regiment, and to accept the dirtiest.

In the latter end of September, the regiment received a route to march to Brabournlees, in the county of Kent; so that we left this brigade-major with his militia regiments, not being sorry at parting with him, whose constant delight consisted in making men miserable.

CHAPTER 3

Leaves Hull

The regiment crossed, the Humber by Barton, and marched to Brigg the first day; but I obtained leave to cross by Grimsby, and called at Louth and Horncastle to see my relations and friends, to whom I soon once more bade *adieu*, in order to join my regiment; and passing the 2nd Division at Deeping, on the 7th October, overtook, at Huntingdon, the 1st division, to which I belonged. We marched from. Huntingdon to St. Neot's Biggleswade, and Hatfield, and arrived at Highgate on the 11th: this was headquarters; but five companies proceeded to Hampstead.

I and a small party of my comrades went forward to Kilbourn, and were quartered at the Red Lion, being only one mile from Hyde Park Corner. After dinner several of our party went to view the metropolis. We walked to St. James's Palace, through the Park and Horse-Guards, and viewed Westminster Bridge and Abbey, together with several places of note, and returned about seven o'clock in the evening, highly delighted with what we had seen.

The next day being Sunday, we halted, and were gratified with another view of the English capital. On Monday morning the regiment marched forward, and about nine o'clock entered London with flying colours, crossed Blackfriars Bridge, and then marched to Bromley, the seat of Sir Thomas Trigg, our head colonel, who met us on the road, dressed in the regimental uniform. The whole of the officers dined with Sir Thomas, who would also have given a treat to the privates, but Lieutenant-Colonel Farley prevented him, fearing the men might conduct themselves improperly if they had too much liberty given them.

The next day we marched to a small town between Maidstone and Bromley, broke into detachments, and went to different villages and public houses on the road. The landlord where I was quartered brought every man a pint of ale, saying, he always behaved well to soldiers, and had never lost any thing by so doing: be added, "I will give every man his dinner, but I cannot accommodate all with beds; but I have plenty of clean straw, and those who will sleep on it shall have a glass of gin each." This piece of liberality so pleased the men, that they vowed they would do anything for such a good and worthy fellow as he.

After dinner, the soldiers began to drink in company with some men and women who had been gathering hops: before night, all were intoxicated, except myself and three others, who retired to repose about nine o'clock, leaving the rest in a state little better than that of madmen. I laid myself down on the chamber floor, with only a rug to cover me; but in about an hour after was disturbed by one of the men running into our room, crying for help, or that we should all be killed. Myself and another, taking up our side-arms and bayonets, after rushing into the bouse, in which we found not one single soldier, forthwith proceeded into the street, where we heard a most dreadful screaming, evidently from a female, and on repairing to the spot whence the cries issued, found that some of the soldiers had laid siege to a farmhouse.

One of the men, with his firelock presented, declared he would fire, if the woman did not open the door of the house: another was kicking at it to break it in: and on inquiring what was the matter, I was told that a country man had stolen a musket, and taken shelter in the house. At length, having succeeded with difficulty in conducting the men away, I returned to my sleeping-room, and lay there laughing at the folly of drunkards; but I had not laid long, before James Bracken, a man of our company, came into the room, drew a bayonet from its scabbard, put it under his coat, and left in haste.

I afterwards learnt that Bracken, who was a papist, had fallen into a dispute with a man called Johnstone, a protestant, and that in the midst of their disputation, the bayonet having fallen from under Bracken's clothes, a battle ensued, in which Johnstone beat his foe completely, and took his weapon from him. In the morning again, as the party was falling in, in order to march and join the regiment on the road, another dispute took place between the same men, and Bracken attempted to stab Johnstone, who instantly raised his musket, and brought his enemy level with the ground, where he lay a considerable time before he came to himself. He was then taken into the public house, and medical assistance was procured, but it was thought his wound would prove mortal.

We left the man under the care of the landlord, and marched Johnstone a prisoner to the regiment: he was then sent to the rear guard; and, when we got to Maidstone, had to lay under the market-cross, instead of being at a public house.—There is not, in many cases, in Ireland, much love lost, on either side, between papist and protestant, and perhaps each has about equal cause for resentment against the other; and accordingly, in the present instance, Johnstone's hatred of the papist may be traced to the circumstance of his father and mother, with some other relations, having been burnt alive by some infuriated Romanists, in the late Irish rebellion, the recollection of which fact must naturally have rankled in Johnstone's mind ever since.

The latter was tried by a court-martial, and sentenced to receive three hundred lashes; but in a few days Bracken recovered, and the other man, having previously borne a good character, was pardoned— I was quartered at the sign of the Castle at Maidstone, the landlord of which was so unfeeling towards our poor women, that he would not allow them to dine with us on any account. In return for this harsh treatment, we put him to all the trouble possible, causing him to provide breakfast, a thing not commonly done.

The next morning, we marched to Lenham: on the 17th we reached Ashford, and on the 18th Brabournlees Barracks, our destined quarters. When at Hull, our regiment was made a light infantry regiment: here we had our regimental clothing altered, and learnt to manoeuvre by the sound of. the bugle, instead of the word of command; and, in conjunction with the 85th, were taught the light infantry exercise and evolutions under the command or direction of General Baron Derottenburgh.

At Christmas our new clothing was ready. It was completely altered, having, instead of shoulder-knots, wings, green tufts in the place of white ones, and bugles in the front of our caps instead of plates. We also gave in our arms and accoutrements, and received in return japanned muskets, with double sights, and a complete set of new accoutrements. One afternoon in April 1809, as two companies were firing ball cartridge, one of the pieces missed fire, and the man who held it, turning round to the rear, as was customary, to examine into the cause of its having only flushed in the pan, the musket immediately exploded, and, dreadful to relate, the ball passed through the body of one of the men that were looking on.

The poor fellow was immediately carried to the hospital, where,

British Light Infantry of the Peninsular War period

notwithstanding the exertions of the regimental and other surgeons, he died, before morning in the greatest agony. His name was Baker; he was a native of the neighbourhood of Lincoln, had about eighty pounds, which he willed to his sister: was buried in the churchyard of Brabournlees, and his funeral was attended by most of the men in our regiment, who much lamented the loss of their worthy comrade.

Brabournlees is a small village: the barracks stood on a common between Ashford and Hythe, and were capable of containing three thousand men: they are five miles from Ashford, seven from Hythe, and twelve from Canterbury, and are pleasantly situated in a fertile country abounding with fruits of various sorts. Whilst at Brabournlees, I received a letter from my brother, informing me of my grandfather's death; he had not forgot me in his will, but left me fifty pounds, to be received when twenty-five years of age. My brother had been so kind as to put half-a-guinea into the seal of his letter, as a present; but, when the letter arrived, I found the seal had been broken open, and the money taken away.

My inquiries at the post-office for the money were quite unsuccessful: upon which I wrote to acquaint my friends at Louth with my misfortune, and they very kindly made up the loss, by sending a post-office draft for the amount lost. Whilst we were here, the 50th Regiment arrived at these barracks, after the retreat and Battle of Corunna, in a very distressed and miserable condition.

In May, an order came that the brigade was to march twelve or fourteen miles twice a week in full marching order, that we might become accustomed to fatigue, a sort of discipline very necessary for us who were expecting every day to be called out on foreign service. I have frequently known some of our men drop in the ranks, as if dead, through excessive beat and fatigue. On one occasion the 68th, 71st, and 85th Regiments marched eight miles, formed line, and manoeuvred on a large common, then marched back to our barracks, hundreds of us not having broken our fast, or eaten anything whatever during the time.

About the 28th of June, the regiment received a route to march to Portsmouth, for embarkation. So urgent was our march, that we were not allowed to halt on Sundays, but marched forced marches until we reached Gosport, and encamped near that place. Various were the reports of the people concerning the object of the expedition: some said it was for one place, and some for another. Nearly all the men of our regiment were lame; for, beside our usual load, sixty rounds of ammunition were added; and, what vexed us worst was, this very ammunition was afterwards taken from us, and fired into the sea by other regiments. It really was a great hardship to be treated in this way.

On the day we arrived at Gosport, Colonel Farley was promoted to the rank of Brigadier-General, and Governor of one of the West-India Islands; and Lieutenant-Colonel Johnson promoted to the full command, and Major Richard Thompson the Second in Command, of the 68th Regiment. Our old commander was an excellent officer, well beloved by his men, who sincerely regretted their loss, which, however, was not badly supplied in the person of Colonel William Johnson, who was an officer that loved his men, and by whom he was respected in return.

The day after Colonel Farley had left us, the regiment was inspected by the general of the division, who expressed his surprise that the men were so lame: the cause being explained, he was satisfied. The general left orders that the regiment was to fire ball cartridge two or three times: accordingly, the next and subsequent days we fired about twenty rounds into the sea. We did not, however, as at other times, fire singly, but by companies and grand Divisions, and, on three or four occasions, volleys of the whole regiment. This was to make us steady, and to prepare us for the time, which was at no great distance, when we should have to engage the enemy in reality. On one occasion, we were firing three deep, and one of the rear-rank men, not looking well along his piece to see that he was clear of his front-rank man, fired, and carried away two fingers and part of the hand of a poor fellow, who was taken with us abroad, and there died. Had he been left in the hospital at Portsmouth, he might most probably have recovered.

In this camp we had a number of canteens and eating houses, or rather tents; but provisions were uncommonly dear: roasted mutton one shilling and nine-pence the pound; beef and other meat in proportion: so that a very little of it fell to my share. About the 13th July, General Baron Derottenburgh arrived, and took the command of the light brigade. As soon as he came into the camp, the whole of our regiment and that of the 85th turned out of their tents, and received the venerable baron with three times three cheers: he beckoned for us to cease, but our respect for him was too great so to do; besides we had no other way of testifying our approbation but by cheering him. He was an able general, and, in every respect, a good officer.

On the 15th, orders came for our, embarkation on the following morning at two o'clock. On Sunday morning, July the 16th, we were ordered to strike the tents, pack them up, and deliver them with our camp utensils into the commissary stores. As soon as this was done, we set fire to the straw; so that the whole country seemed to be in a blaze. Our colonel reprimanded us for this freak; but he was too late, for all the straw that could be found was already consumed. At daylight the bugles sounded: the regiment then formed, and moved off towards the place of embarkation, which was on the Gosport side of the water: when we arrived at the water-side, the boats were ready to receive us.

We then embarked by companies: the men were in high spirits, and gave three cheers as they left the shore, the bugles and band playing until the regiment reached the *Caesar*, of ninety guns. But, oh! what an affecting scene took place between the married men and their families! It was truly distressing to see the anguish of the poor women at parting, some of whom were nearly frantic, others fainting away, and their children crying by their sides or in their arms, so that the hardest heart must have been moved at the sight. Many of these pitiable, creatures never saw their husbands more; and even before six weeks had passed over numbers of them were widows, and their children orphans.

On this occasion my feelings nearly overcame me, and I really could not help rejoicing that I was a single man. If such, then, were the acuteness of the feelings of a mere looker-on, what must have been the feelings of the poor men themselves who had to be actors in the heartrending scene!

The whole of our regiment was put on board the *Caesar*, which mounted ninety guns: her lower-deck guns had been taken out to make room for the troops. We were nine hundred strong; the ship's company about six hundred, besides officers; making, in all, nearly, one thousand five hundred and fifty men on board of this massy vessel. The name of the captain of the *Caesar* was Richardson, a very humane and good commander.

We lay at Spithead until the morning of the 27th, when, we weighed anchor and set sail: and, on Friday evening the 28th, arrived in the Downs. Here the fleet had collected in great force, for the purpose of sailing with the expedition to the island of Walcheren. Early on Saturday morning, the fleet sailed in three divisions, one division at three o'clock, the other at four, and the last, the one I was in, about five o'clock.

The fleet was so large that we could not all get on our way together: it was, perhaps, one of the largest fleets that has left England for many years, there being, no less than sixty thousand troops on board, and nearly, twenty thousand sailors and marines; making altogether about eighty thousand effective men. About nine o'clock on Saturday evening we let go our anchor within six miles of the shores of the island of Walcheren. During the night, a vessel ran foul of the *Caesar*, which caused a terrible shock, but no damage was done to either vessel.

Next morning, we weighed anchor, and sailed towards the north point of this island, in order to effect a landing: our vessel, ran aground with such violence, that at first it was thought she would have gone to pieces; but after straining herself very much, she was got off. The soldiers were fastened below, in order to prevent confusion. We at length got to our destination, and began to prepare for landing: all the flat-bottomed boats in the fleet were put in readiness: each boat had a cannonade fixed in its bow, and was manned with a proper number of men to fire, if occasion should require it.

The whole of the boats belonging to the men of war and transports having got to their respective stations, and received the troops, they began to collect by regiments, and formed a line of boats, which reached a great distance. Each of the larger boats had a flag: the sight was uncommonly grand, and had an imposing effect. By this time a number of gunboats had collected to cover the landing: at length the signal was given for the boats to advance to the shore in line; in doing which the only annoyance they met with was from a battery of three guns. The troops had no sooner effected a landing, which they did in good order, and without loss, than they routed the enemy from their battery, and caused them to fly in confusion.

With the first division that landed, were a number of sailors, who pursued the enemy a considerable distance, and greatly annoyed them. It now became our turn to land; the regiment having received three days' provisions, sixty round of ammunition each, and a store of good flints, together with a supply of liquor. We accordingly stepped into the boats, and landed without an accident, about eight o'clock on Sunday evening the 30th July 1809, and were compelled to lay all night on the sand, without a tent, or any other covering to protect us from the night air. We had left our knapsacks on board, having only our haversacks, canteens, and rolled coats with us.

We remained on the sand-hill until the afternoon of the 31st. I had never seen anything to equal the appearance of our army before: it reached about four miles along these hills. In the afternoon, our company, with part of another, and forty of the 95th Rifle Corps; making in all about two hundred, were sent to join General Graham's brigade, consisting of the 3rd battalion of the 1st Royals, the 5th and 35th Regiments. We were to act as riflemen to this brigade of heavy infantry. Towards evening we went in quest of the enemy, and formed two or three times to attack their outposts, but they retreated without being brought to action.

That night we slept in the streets of a small village, but had a very strong guard and piquets to look out for the enemy, who were not more than about a mile from us. The next morning, we advanced at the head of the brigade, but had not proceeded far, before we discovered a battery, and several men standing at the guns. General Graham ordered the column to halt, and then sent to know who they were, When the party approached, the men ran off from the guns: they turned out to be only a number of country people, who were frightened at the approach of our brigade. The column advanced until it reached the sand-hills to the west of Flushing, and these found the enemy ready prepared to receive us.

Our cannon was ordered forward, and several shots were fired upon the foe. A number of the enemy were sheltered in a wood to our left; General Graham ordered the cannon to be turned, and to commence firing into it: he also sent a party to dislodge the enemy, and to force them into the main road. At this time the light troops were ordered forward, and in a few minutes, we were, for the first time, engaged with the French Army; for, I believe nine-tenths, at least, of our regiment had never been engaged before. The first onset very much terrified me; but gradually, my fears subsided, and I became calm and, deliberate. We fought along the sand-hills for seven miles, and took several batteries mounted with brass guns.

One of the magazines blew up, and caused a tremendous shock, something like an earthquake. To the right, between the sea and the hills, were a number of piles, in ranks, nearly as high as men, and which had the appearance of soldiers at a distance. Several of us fired at them, thinking they were the enemy, but we soon discovered our mistake: yet we afterwards found we had not fired altogether in vain; for there was a poor Frenchman laid behind the piles, with his brains blown out, and lying in his cap. Shortly we came within the range of the Flushing batteries; but their own men being between us and the town, the guns were as yet silent.

I entered a house for a drink; and these beheld a sight, which affords some idea of the shocking devastation that must always mark a country which has the misfortune to become the seat of war. It being a dairy farm-house, there was standing in a room a large tub of butter-milk, but such was the hurry and confusion of the soldiers who had been there before me, that they had broken every vessel in the house, and the room was literally up to the ankles in butter-milk; and not one whole vessel remained to drink it out with. With great; difficulty, however, I got my canteen full of milk and cider, and then ran after the party.

About this time, the cannon from the garrison began to play upon us with great fury. As I was going along, I had to pass a flag-staff and signal-post full of blocks and tackles. Scarcely had I got under it, when a twenty-four-pound shot from the battery struck the flag-staff, and killed and wounded several of the soldiers that were marching under the hill. Their cries were dreadful. A little further on a soldier of the 5th Regiment received a cannon-shot through the centre of his body, which, as he laid upon the earth, presented a horrid spectacle; for we could see the ground through his carcase.

Still advancing along, I perceived a man walking on the brow of a rising ground, when suddenly a shot came, struck the ground about ten inches below his feet, knocked up his heels, and sent him rolling down the hill, at the bottom of which he got upon his legs again, and ran after his regiment, not having received any injury whatever. As soon as we arrived at the end of the hills, we were obliged to stop; for, by passing the corner, we should have exposed ourselves to the main battery of the enemy. As it was, the carnage was dreadful. Out of the grenadier companies of our brigade alone lost forty men, killed and wounded; therefore, the loss of the three regiments could not fail to have been very great had we not sheltered ourselves in this spot. About this time one of General Graham's *aide-de-camps* received a very severe wound, and was carried to the rear: the loss of the light troops, however, was comparatively small, although at the head of the brigade, and in every way exposed to the enemy's fire.

The loss sustained by our company was about ten wounded: be-ing light infantry, we took every advantage; while the heavy troops were necessarily exposed, having to keep their ranks, and to follow as our supports. There was with us a man called Murphy, who had long wished he might be killed, in the first engagement: his wish was partly granted, for he received a severe wound, and had to undergo an amputation near the shoulder. After we had driven the enemy into the town, I and three others were sent to bury the dead, and to take care of the wounded men; but when we came to the places we found the dead had already been buried, and the wounded as well taken care of as circumstances would admit.

In returning to our company, we had to run over an open ground that was completely exposed to the main battery of the enemy's garrison; but we passed over it without any injury whatever, although we had some very narrow escapes indeed. On the left flank of our company was an orchard, with a barn standing near it, upon which the enemy kept such a heavy fire, that Colonel Hay thought prudent to have it destroyed, and sent orders to Captain Hawkins to see that it was done. The barn was accordingly set on fire, and consumed to ashes. There were two calves consumed with it: the sufferings of these dumb animals were great, and affected the captain even to tears: had he known beforehand that they were in the barn, every effort would have been made to rescue them.

The evening coming on, the firing ceased on both sides; but we had strong guards and piquets in our front, to watch the motions of the enemy. Captain Hawkins gave orders for his men to form in an open field, and for every other man to keep awake, the rest to lay down; but it was with difficulty that any of us, after the fatigues of the day, could keep awake. About midnight a supply of bread arrived, and each man received his allowance, also a small quantity of raw bacon and onions, which were very acceptable.

Soon after daylight in the morning, a party of the enemy made an attempt to take some of our guns. We charged them nearly to the walls of the garrison, and took several prisoners, amongst whom was a French officer, who would not give up his sword to one of the First Royals: the soldier instantly lifted up his musket, and ran the unfortunate officer through the body with his bayonet, exclaiming at the same time, "I will send your soul to the devil!" Our officers did not approve of this savage act of cruelly; for although the soldier might by some be considered as having done his duty, and even as a hero into the bargain, yet he was, undoubtedly, a hardened monster, and no man of a right mind or of true bravery would say that heroism consists in such conduct.

After thus repulsing the enemy and driving them back into the town, the cannon and mortars from their batteries opened a most tremendous fire, which continued for some time; but we, being partly sheltered in the ditches, did not on this occasion sustain any serious injury. The enemy at this time had a strong piquet under cover of their guns, who kept up a constant discharge of musketry, the balls of which whistled over our heads, sometimes lodging in the trees, and cutting the small branches, so that we were compelled to remain close to the banks for safety. It is not usual to relieve the advanced posts by daylight, but at one o'clock the relief came, and we were ordered to the rear about two miles, to cook our provisions, and to rest for the night.

By some means or other the enemy learnt that the guards and piquets were relieving, and instantly opened a fire upon us hotter if possible than ever, and, I am sorry to say, not without doing some execution on our men. This compelled us to retreat to the rear one by one, or the consequences might have been much worse; for their cannon could reach us a mile in the rear of the advanced posts; so that all the time we were retreating our backs were exposed until we had got out of the range of their battery. I at length arrived in safety at our little camp, received my provisions, cooked them, and had a good night's rest in the open air. Here we lay until the next evening, and then joined the main body of our regiment, which was encamped about one mile to the right of the Middleburgh road, and only just out of the reach of the enemy's cannon, the shot frequently falling within one hundred yards of the camp ground.

When the party joined the regiment, great was our grief on hearing that several of our best comrades were no more. The main body of the regiment, with a part of the 85th, drove the enemy before them on the Middleburgh road, and advanced to the very gates of Flushing, at which point our colonel, hoping to secure possession of the drawbridge, made a vigorous push, and was within two minutes of doing it, but the enemy drew up the bridge in time to save it, and thus left the 68th and part of the 85th Regiments exposed to the shot, shell, and musketry of the garrison, which did considerable execution. We had one man wounded at the gate of the town: the enemy took him into their hospital, and used him very well.

There was not much praise due to our commander on this occasion; his courage certainly was great, but he might have lost the most of his regiment by this rash effort. After this, the regiment was employed in building batteries and throwing up breastworks and trenches, and continued occupied in this way until the works were completed.

CHAPTER 4

Fatal Disease Among the Troops

There was from our camp a narrow lane, fenced on each side by a quick hedge: this lane was very straight, and two of the enemy's guns commanded it, which greatly annoyed us, but, in order to protect ourselves from their destructive fire, we built in the lane walls made of bags filled with earth, and these walls extending from opposite sides of the lane, but not quite across it, and being placed in alternate opposition, instead of exactly facing each other, left a passage sufficiently wide for the troops to pass and re-pass, something in this way:

One night, as we were finishing a battery of twelve guns, one of our men, named Duffin, fell from the top of it into the pond in front of the works, and was with difficulty taken up, but he sustained no injury, more than getting wet. Whilst we were in our camp, a corporal of Captain Gough's company, who had been accused of cowardice, was led by the colonel in front of each company at the morning parade, the colonel saying as he passed, "Soldiers, behold a coward!" The corporal was then taken in front of the whole regiment, his stripes were taken off, and he was sent ignominiously to his company as a private. I have heard it said, that he was not to blame, but that an officer was the guilty person, who had contrived to blame the poor corporal—One day, while employed in building batteries, trenches, and other works, a bomb-shell fell on an old house: it burst, and our first major being near it, was wounded in the right arm, and obliged to undergo amputation very near the shoulder.

About the 12th August everything was in readiness for commencing the bombardment; the bomb vessels were ordered to be ready to co-operate with the land batteries: in the afternoon of the 13th, being Sunday, the batteries opened upon the town, though partially, until about nine o'clock at night. Our regiment was in readiness to act in case of a *sorté*. Between nine and ten the thunder of our battering guns was terrible: the guns of the enemy were not altogether silent. There was a mortar battery near us, from which the shells were thrown as fast as possible; and at intervals we could hear the dreadful cries of the inhabitants from the town.

Lord Chatham had, previous to the commencement of the bombardment, given leave for the inhabitants to quit the town; but the French governor would not allow it, and, in consequence, hundreds of the poor people were killed and wounded. No one can conceive the horrors of a bombardment, without witnessing them: on this very night I saw from twelve to sixteen bomb shells in the air together; and, at the same time, from thirty to forty cannon-shots were thrown into the town, which destroyed houses, churches, and everything far and near: but what astonished me the most were the Congreve rockets, which I had never seen fired before, and which, when the rocket battery began to play, completely illuminated the air, and presented a very grand and curious appearance. (*Vide The Details of the Rocket System Employed by the British Army During the Napoleonic Wars* by William Congreve, Congreve's own work on the effectiveness and operation of his rockets: Leonaur 2021.)

The rockets had not played more than fifteen minutes, before one of the churches caught fire, and in a little time was in a complete blaze. The cannons, mortars, and rockets from the land batteries, together with the dreadful bombardment from the shipping, continued to play all night, and did not cease until about two o'clock on Monday afternoon. During this period, some of our batteries were so burned, that it was found necessary to repair them: however, being made of nothing but kids staked down and filled with earth, they were soon repaired and put into good condition. Soon afterwards the enemy sent a truce, with terms of capitulation; but these terms were not acceded to.

There was a thorough stillness on both sides during the whole of the afternoon, and until about twelve o'clock at night, when our batteries opened as they had never done before, and continued to play upon the town for several hours; but at length the governor sent conditions, and offered to surrender, promising that the troops under his command should, within a specified time be marched out of the garrison with the honours of war; the officers to retain their personal property, and the soldiers their knapsacks. These conditions were accepted by the British commander; and, on the morning of the 15th August, the British Army was put in motion, and assembled on the right of the town, in order to receive the French garrison as they marched out.

In a few hours, the bands and drums of the enemy saluted our ears, and the enemy themselves soon afterwards appeared with two pieces of cannon, the governor and generals riding at the head of their men, every one of the latter bearing his musket, and the officers their drawn swords, the regimental colours flying at the same time—a sight altogether exceedingly sublime. They marched to the beach, and there laid down their arms, of which we took possession, and put them into the military stores. The whole of the French soldiery of the garrison were embarked on board a part of the fleet, and sent to England prisoners of war.

After having embarked the enemy, we returned to our camp with light hearts, highly gratified with our success in having taken this very formidable fortification, a work, the execution of which, including the labour of building batteries, throwing up trenches, and reducing this stronghold itself, occupied us only about twelve, days. Although close to the gates, I never was in the town of Flushing, which is situated on the north bank of the western Scheldt, and is surrounded by a deep ditch filled with water, very wide and deep. The ramparts wore a beautiful appearance, being covered with grass; but the houses and barracks looked dismal indeed.

The island of Walcheren is nine miles long, and eight broad; the soil is very fertile, producing all the kinds of grain, vegetables, and fruits that are grown in England; but the island being low, is subject to frequent inundations; indeed the enemy had made an attempt to flood it during the siege, but were frustrated in their design.

About three days after the surrender of Flushing, the regiment received orders to march to South Beveland, and accordingly, proceeded through Middleburgh, which is the capital of this island, and one of the most delightful towns I ever saw, everything appearing clean and neat, and the houses and shops being decorated in a very beautiful manner. I could understand the language of the inhabitants almost as well as my own, for hundreds of their words were, so near to ours in sound and meaning, that we could not possibly misapply theirs.

We arrived at a certain place on the River Scheldt, and were conveyed in boats over into the island of South Beveland, and took up our quarters in three small villages near Goes, the capital of Beveland, where we remained, about three weeks. Whilst in these villages we had a man punished for stealing two or three apples, our officers being very severe. In this island milk was very cheap: I have bought a puncheon full of good milk for six *doits*, equal to three farthings English money. Potatoes, onions, bread, butter, cheese, coffee, tobacco, Hollands and beer, were also very cheap and plentiful: indeed, this expedition was altogether well supplied with provisions and military stoves of every description.

But, although the army suffered nothing from the want of the necessaries of life, yet they suffered greatly in another way; for, in the beginning of September, a dreadful and fatal disease, being an intermitting fever and ague, and not unlike the fen ague, broke out amongst them, and several of the men died daily. I was amongst the first that were attacked by this disease, and laid some days in a barn, without partaking of any food whatever, and was brought so exceedingly low, that I was almost insensible to anything that was going on amongst my comrades.

I was at length taken to an hospital about three miles distant, where the sick had been collected in great numbers. The first night of my being there, a Roman Catholic priest came to absolve a man of our regiment who was in a dying state, and paid great attention to the poor man: after having absolved him, he advised us to abstain from drinking cold water, or eating too much fruit, and we could not but respect the good priest for his advice.

The horrors of this place caused me in some measure to forget my own complaint, or nearly so; and I thought, to be sure, I must die, if I remained much longer in this doleful barn. The next day the doctors came round to visit their patients: I and three others said we were better, but we must have been deceived and mislead by our feelings, excited as they were by the terrible scene around us. The doctors therefore ordered that we should be taken in a waggon to another barn about four miles distant; but still there I was no better, but rather worse, and though I felt no pain, yet was always low and feeble, wasting away, until my body was reduced to a mere skeleton.

At last, an order came for the regiment to march to Tervere, in the north of the island of Walcheren: the wagons came, and the sick men were put into them; at which time I was so weak, that I could not help myself. After a tedious journey, we arrived at the ferry where boats were in readiness to take us over the River Scheldt; in passing which it was my misfortune to lose my knapsack, and everything belonging me, except an old shirt. From this point we soon reached Tervere General Hospital, which was in a large church, at the very threshold of which, as I entered, I saw the corpses of two soldiers lying on the floor, with their feet uncovered, a sight that made me so sick and ill, that I thought I should have fainted.

So much was my mind affected by this sad scene, that had I been in the possession of a thousand worlds, I would have given them at that moment to have been in any part of old England. We were soon provided with comfortable beds and bedding, and, receiving a proper diet, I began to recover; but one afternoon, a man of our regiment set about washing his shirt, and three of us imprudently followed his example, for which we were severely punished, every one of us being taken the same evening with a relapse of the ague, which continued to shake us every day for several weeks.

I believe, I did not eat one pound of bread for eighteen days: I had my senses frequently taken from me, and, undoubtedly, must have given up at past recovery. At length orders came for the sick men to be embarked for England: the doctors came round to select those whom they thought capable of being removed, and I was one of the number. The joyful news infused new life into me; and the next day we were put on board a transport, which had been fitted up for the purpose.

I really was pleased to leave this place, for it was dreadful to see the poor men dying. I have known nine men die out of our hospital, and from twenty to thirty be interred, daily, and from the different hospitals: so that this enemy was actually worse than the united French Army, with all their guns, mortars, and instruments of death put together; for our regiment lost only ninety in killed and wounded, at the taking of Flushing; but this foe actually destroyed more than three hundred of our brave and well-disciplined comrades, besides leaving a great number more in such a state as made them forever unfit for service again.

I never knew what disease was, until I had the Flushing sickness, of which I was ill twelve months. It was the opinion of medical men, that those who were afflicted by this disorder would never recover, or be so well as they had been before: this might be the case in some instances; but many of our men recovered, and afterwards passed through the fatigues of war, not having one day's sickness.

We lay at anchor in the harbour about three days; but the heat of the transport, being so crowded with men, had a bad effect on us; however, the thought of once more seeing our native land caused us to put up with every inconvenience cheerfully sand contentedly.

About the 10th October we weighed anchor and left the island of

Walcheren. On our passage nothing remarkable occurred. One of my comrades died, and I was present when the funeral service was read over him; in which, instead of saying, "We therefore commit his body to the ground," it was, "We therefore commit his body to the deep." When the corpse was lowered into the sea, I had some of the most unpleasant and uncomfortable feelings imaginable; and was so much affected, that I thought I should never look up again.

He was only about twenty years of age: what must have been the anguish of his poor mother, when she heard the distressing news that her son was no more! But I forbear further expressions of commiseration for this event, which was only one amongst thousands of others that would wring the hearts of parents and widows thus miserably deprived of their sons and husbands forever. Oh! The horrors and devastations of war, when shall they have an end!

About the 15th we got within sight of England, the sweet and delightful land of our homes, and towards evening dropped anchor opposite Dover, in Kent. How comfortable were my feelings, under the reflection, that I had once more reached my native shores! Sleep scarcely closed my eyes during the night, on account of the constant rush of ideas that passed through my mind as it dwelt, at some times, on the pleasure that I was now about to reap in the society of my relatives at home, and, at others, on the scenes of distress and danger which I and my companions in arms had been witness of, and actors in during the late expedition to Walcheren.

In the morning we disembarked, marched up to Dover Castle, and took up our quarters in the barracks, which appeared like a palace, to what we had been accustomed during the last four months, and from the time of our leaving Brabournlees to this period.

CHAPTER 5

Furlough to Louth

By this time, I had recovered a deal of my strength, and therefore made use of this opportunity of viewing the ancient castle and works of this fortification. The barracks are capable of containing three thousand men, with a sufficient quantity of provision and stores, for a seven years' siege. In this place stands the celebrated Queen Anne's pocket-piece, a cannon which, it is said, would carry a ball from Dover to Calais twenty-one miles. Whether the statement be true or false I cannot say; but this I know, that it is about twenty-four feet long, and will carry a nine-pound ball: at present, it is in such a state that it cannot be fired.

From the castle we had a clear view into France, which is not more than twenty-one miles off, and, from low water to low water, the distance is not more than nineteen miles—Dover contains a population of from sixteen to eighteen thousand inhabitants, and is the constant resort of foreigners passing and repassing to and from every part of the continent, but especially from France.

About the 20th an order came for our removal to the regimental depot at Brabournlees barracks. The first day we reached Folkstone; the second, Hythe; and, on the third, we arrived at the peaceful and healthy village of Brabournlees, where we were heartily welcomed by the officers and soldiers of the depot. We were put into comfortable barracks, and in every respect well taken care of; for at this time, we were looked upon as something more than those who had stayed at home.

On the 25th we celebrated the jubilee of the accession of George III., every man receiving half-a-crown in advance to help him to keep the festival: it was a day of great rejoicing with us, and while we amused ourselves in recounting the numerous incidents of the expedition to Flushing, I even began to think that my sufferings were over;

but indeed, they had scarcely begun, for, on the 26th of October I had a relapse of the disease. The ague attacked me every day, my appetite left me, and I lay four days in the barrack-room unable to partake of food, sometimes shaking with cold, and at others burning with fever and heat, without power to raise my head, or to lift myself in my bed.

On the evening of the fourth day, I was removed to the hospital of Brabournlees, where the sick of the 71st, 85th, and 68th Regiments were attended by medical officers: the doctor who attended our ward belonged to the Royal South Lincoln Militia. In this doleful place I was confined by sickness for a considerable time. The sick men from Flushing, continued arrive, until the hospital was crowded with patients belonging to the three regiments above mentioned.

Death began to make its way amongst us: three out of our ward were no more, and I was given up by all the medical men in the hospital; and for my own part, I certainly expected to have gone the way of all flesh; but, as the last resource, the doctor prescribed for me one pint of port wine per day, and at this time, too, as luck would have it, my good friends at Louth sent me a small present in cash, which helped me greatly, so that I began to recover, and on the 20th quitted the hospital and joined the depot. I had not, however, been long there, before I was ordered to attend the funeral of one of our regiment as a bearer, and had to assist in carrying the corpse above a mile; and, oh! how miserable were my reflections: no one to shed a tear of pity, or to heave a sigh over the poor dead man! I felt, but could not weep, because things of this kind were so frequently taking place, especially at this fatal period, that I had learnt to look upon them with dry eyes.

About this time, I applied to the commanding officer for a furlough, saying, that my own country air might do me good; and, having obtained leave of absence for forty-two days, and received my money, started on my way, but had no sooner reached Ashford, than my old complaint, the ague, returned, and gave me a terrible shaking at the canteen of the barracks there. Having nothing but my old clothing on my person, I was ashamed to call at respectable houses for lodgings; I therefore, after my fit was over, proceeded to a small village two miles distant, and took up my quarters at the sign of the Coach and Horses, but continued to be very unwell during the night.

The next morning, I took coach for London, but, before we reached Maidstone, a severe fit of the ague beset me, whereupon a lady prevailed with the coachman to allow me to get inside, and, after I had taken my seat there, kindly offered me brandy. After passing another dreadful night, I next morning took a place, by mistake, in the Stilton, instead of the Boston, coach. This day again the ague visited me, and gave me a desperate shaking during the journey; but some gentlemen put me inside, and behaved exceedingly well to me. They asked me several questions relative to the late expedition, and I found that one of them was a captain of a transport, having been engaged in carrying troops and stores to and from Flushing: he was remarkably kind to me.

At one in the morning, we arrived at Stilton: the horses were immediately changed, and the coach started for Stamford; but in consequence of my mistake I could proceed no farther in this conveyance. The night was extremely cold and stormy, and I would gladly have laid myself down in a stable; but finding all the doors closed, I entered the Angel Inn yard, and, for want of a better berth, opened the door of one of the chaises there; I stepped in, and, pulling up the windows, laid down in the body of the chaise, in which situation, packed and rolled up, though my limbs were, like a salmon in a kit, in not the most easy posture in the world, I slept well until eight o'clock, when I roused myself, and letting down the window, and popping my head out, inquired what o'clock it was. "I will clock you, you rascal!" exclaimed one of the ostlers.

Looking very steadfastly at him, "Yes, and I will make some of you smart for leaving me in the street, exposed in the rain and cold," answered I; and immediately got out of the chaise. My answer was in an unexpected tone, and none of the ostlers dared to say another word. I then repaired to the sign of the Wheat Sheaf, and ordered breakfast; and there a woman, moved with a sight of my condition, gave me a shilling, saying, that her husband was in the army.

The same day, at Norman-Cross barracks, the place where the French prisoners were confined, the driver of a provision-wagon, which was coming out of the barrack-yard as I passed, allowed me to ride to Peterborough with him, not charging me anything., This was the first day of my journey in which I had not a fit of the ague. On this and the succeeding days I passed through Spalding and Swineshead, partly on foot, and partly by waggon, not without meeting with many difficulties on the road. From Swineshead, the next morning I started for Langret Ferry, and arrived there after a severe march of six miles on a road so exceedingly bad, that I stuck fast in the clay and mire several times; being very weak, it was with the greatest difficulty I weathered through.

Finding good quarters at an inn there, and being very tired, I thought I could not do better than remain during the night at so hospitable a house: all the company took notice of me, and offered me drink. One person asked whether I had not a brother called William Green and being answered in the affirmative, "I know him very well," said he, "and, for his sake, will see that you do not want for anything during your stay in this place." Indeed, such was the kindness of the company, that some of them got to fighting on my account; for having quitted my seat for a moment, a person took possession of it during my absence, and another of the company quarrelled with the intruder, and fought him for imposing upon a poor and sick soldier.

The landlord would not even draw any more ale for the man, because he conceived I had been ill used by him. I got a good supper, slept in a good bed, and partook of a good breakfast, after which I started for Horncastle, the landlord putting me into the best road. He would not take anything for my supper, bed, or breakfast; but sent me off, wishing me well home to my friends.

I travelled slowly along the bank of the Witham, and arrived at Dogdike about noon: the hostess was so kind that she gave me my dinner: the company in this place also were kind unto me. An old man, who was full of his quirks and catches, said, he would keep me a fortnight upon roast beef and ale if I would go with him. I gave the old gentleman such answers to his questions as highly delighted the company; so that they would have given me anything whilst I remained amongst them.

Leaving this place, I proceeded to Coningsby and Horncastle; and in visits amongst friends at those two towns spent twelve days more: and then, with high expectations, went forward to Louth. As soon as I reached the top of Calkwell Hill, and got a glance of the lofty spire of Louth church, my feelings were such that I cannot describe them; and surely none but those who have been in like circumstances can imagine how delighted I was once more to see (what I may consider) my native place.

My heart beat, my feelings ran high, and it was with difficulty I contained myself: I thought of this and the other acquaintance; but most of my grandmother, Widow Cuthbert; and my aunt, Ann Green: these were my principal friends, to whom I looked for help and assistance; indeed, I could rely with confidence on both these sources for every assistance I wanted in this time of need and necessity. Oh! with what transports of joy did I think of my friends and relations! I thought, to see them and to enjoy their society would make me completely happy. It will not be wondered that I should have had these acute feelings, when we take into account my age, being only nineteen, and being so afflicted and broken down by the Flushing sickness.

At length I arrived at the end of the town, and was so eager to see my friends, that I knew not whom to visit first; but my affection led me to the Quarry. The moment I entered the house, my grandmother made me heartily welcome; and I really felt that I was at home. She soon got me some refreshment: after I had partaken of it, I went down, ill as I was, into the town, and visited all my relations, and then returned to the Quarry, and perhaps for the first time knew the delightful pleasures of home. I retired to rest and slept soundly, not having the dreadful roar of the cannon of Flushing to disturb me, nor the moans of the dying soldiers in the hospitals to harrow up my feelings: no, all was peace.

I had no father or mother, or my feelings might have been different; but, as it was, I had as much rejoicing in my mind over my relatives as though they had been nearer to me, and I shall for ever have to acknowledge their goodness and kindness to me, who had merited nothing from them but their displeasure. Even my old master Foggitt did not slight me, but behaved very kindly; as did several of my old shop-mates.

As the expiration of my furlough approached, although I had obtained an addition to it of thirty-one days, in consequence of another severe attack of the ague, yet so much were my feelings alienated from war-like adventures, partly by the sweets of home, now dearer to me than ever, and more than all by my reflections on the scenes of the Flushing expedition, and the sufferings I had undergone in the hospital, which were now constantly rushing on my mind, that I dreaded the time of my departure again.

At length the last day came, and I almost repented having come home at all. Various were the unhappy feelings which passed in my mind through the day, but more so during the night. The morning came: I arose with unpleasant sensations, and repaired to the town to take leave of my friends, thinking I should never see them again, both my grandmother and my aunt being above eighty years of age. Oh! with what reluctance did I leave my friends, and the delightful town of Louth! I looked behind me several times, and said in my mind, I shall never visit it again.

CHAPTER 6

I Again Join the Regiment

I arrived at Horncastle about two o'clock. My friends there would have me remain a few days with them, for which purpose my leave of absence was prolonged eight days more; at the expiration of which I left Horncastle, called at Coningsby, and then proceeded to Boston, to pay a visit to my brother. After spending a few happy days with him, I left Boston, in order to join my regiment, then laying at Brabourn-lees barracks. The first day I reached Deeping; the second, Stilton; and on the fourth, London; I passed through, and took up my quarters at Newcross.

Next morning I started for Maidstone, but was taken ill of the ague at a village on the road, and was obliged to go to bed, being so exceedingly ill that I was alarmed lest my old complaint should return: but the next morning I was able to march, and passing through Maidstone, took up my quarters at Lenham; and on the following day arrived at Ashford, which is only five miles from Brabournlees; and the next morning, after purchasing several necessaries, joined my regiment.

I left the army at Tervere, in the island of Walcheren, at the period when the fever was most fatal. The 68th Regiment was completely altered, nearly four hundred having died of the disease, besides what were killed and wounded at the siege and bombardment of Flushing, and at this time several of the men were in the hospital very ill of the ague, and many deaths occurred. Notwithstanding the mortality which had taken place, I found several of my old comrades, who were ready to join my company; and I was really glad to see those again who had been my companions in the fatigues of war.

The regiment remained at Brabournlees until the month of March, when we were ordered to Hythe, distant only seven miles. The barracks stand on a very high hill, whence we had a view into France, which could be seen very well in clear weather. The troops

51

lying at this place were as follows: the 68th, Second Battalion of the 95th Rifle Corps, the Devonshire Militia, and the Royal Staff Corps, whose barracks were like a palace. The brigade was under the command of a general who was uncommonly strict: on one occasion he confined the whole of the three regiments to their barracks, ordering a piquet of twenty-one men from each regiment to patrol the streets and neighbourhood of Hythe every hour, and to take up every soldier who dared to leave the barracks, or disobey the general's orders.

About this time, we had a grand field-day on the heights near Sandgate: the troops present were the 68th, 95th, the Devonshire Militia, a regiment which lay in the Cliff barracks, and the 85th, which had marched from Brabournlees, ten miles, in heavy marching order, hundreds of them probably not having broken their fast. We then fought a sham engagement, and manoeuvred several hours; after which we marched to our respective barracks. The 85th Regiment must have suffered greatly during the excessive fatigues of the day: our regiment had no knapsacks, and had only three miles to march home; yet we were nearly exhausted. What then must have been their condition who had marched twenty miles, and gone through the manoeuvres of a field-day, many of them fasting until evening.

Whilst we laid at Hythe, our bugle-major died of the Walcheren sickness, and over him was held what is called an Irish Wake. To me it appeared so ridiculous, that I know not how to reconcile it to reason and religion. I belonged to the same company as the deceased, and lived in the same room: he was a married man, and died in his barrack-room, a thing not common in the regular army; but he and his wife being favourites, were allowed the privilege of remaining in the barrack-room during his illness. The wake lasted two nights, on which occasion. We had much smoking and drinking, different Irish games were played, and tales were told, and thus the nights were spent: there was no restraint whatever, so that the wake resembled a wedding rather than anything else. The bugle-major was a very promising young man, and was respected by all who knew him: his wife's father was a native of Bourn in this county, and had been in the 68th above thirty years.

About the 9th April an express arrived with orders for the regiment to be in readiness to march at a moment's notice to London, to quell the disturbance occasioned by the committal of Sir Francis Burdett to the Tower. Every man received flints, and ammunition was in readiness to be served out: we were kept in suspense three days, not daring to leave the barracks for more than twenty minutes together. Several regiments near London were put in motion; but we being sixty-eight miles from the Metropolis, never left our barracks.

Nothing of importance happened to the regiment for a considerable time. A circumstance, however, transpired, which I must not omit to relate: one of the captains kept a mistress, who, for some error in her conduct, was turned off: the result was most painful; for the poor creature put an end to her existence, by taking poison. She was not more than twenty years of age, and most probably had been seduced from her friends in London. The jury brought in a verdict of lunacy, and she was buried in Hythe churchyard, pitied by all who knew her: thus perished this beautiful young female in the bloom of life.

About this period government gave orders that a school should be established in each regiment, for the laudable purpose of teaching the young men and soldiers' children to read and write, allowing ten ponds, a year to the master. Into this school I entered, and in a little time was reckoned the first scholar in it: the colonel allowed us the whole of each afternoon to improve in reading, writings &c. I took great delight in this employment, and I only regret that the school did not commence sooner. I am, however, greatly indebted to this valuable measure of our then excellent Commander in Chief, His late Royal Highness the Duke of York.

In September, Major Thompson parted with his servant in consequence of a disagreement. My steady conduct, and attention to the school, induced the major to select me to be his successor. I apologised, saying, "I have never been a servant, nor am I at all acquainted with the duty you will require from me."

"Never mind that," said he; "I like you the better for it; I will teach you myself."

I accordingly went with him: he then gave me the keys, and I waited upon him and his partner at dinner. I have stated before that the major had lost one arm; so that I had to be in constant attendance, for he could neither dress nor undress without assistance. Whilst with him, I had the greatest plenty of everything, and was never more happy or contented in my life: the major was a man of honour and principle, and delighted to see me comfortable, for which reason he gave me a beautiful suit of clothes, a great coat worth five pounds, with several other necessaries, and liberty to read the books of the circulating library: even when he was on leave of absence, I had the same privilege allowed me.

About the 26th November, 1810, it began to be reported that we were soon to embark for Spain, and in December we received a route for that purpose. The first day we marched to Rye, our baggage and men being conveyed part of the way, in boats on the new royal canal. I was quartered at the head inn, but my master went forward to the next stage: the second day we arrived at Battle, after marching through rain and storm nearly all the day, the poor women and children on the baggage-waggons being almost lost. The third day we reached Hailsham; the fourth, Lewes; and on the fifth, Little Hampton.

Three companies were sent to Arundel, two to Bognor, and five remained at Little Hampton, the headquarters of the regiment. Colonel Johnson being on leave of absence, the command devolved upon my master. I suppose it was intended that we should have gone forward to Portsmouth, and embarked; but some delay took place, so that we halted in this beautiful part of the county of Sussex—Little Hampton is a sea-port and watering place, containing several good buildings, and excellent accommodations for sea bathers: the barracks were very comfortable, and would contain about four hundred men: here we spent the Christmas of 1810.

About this time a very serious affray took place between the inhabitants of Arundel and a few men belonging to the detachment of our regiment stationed there. Several young men were in the constant habit of insulting the officers as they passed along the streets: being determined to resent these repeated insults, the officers took along with them, on a night agreed upon, a sergeant and several privates, and, dashing into the town, commenced hostilities: the officers and men being armed with heavy sticks, laid on all they met; so that in a few minutes all was dismay and confusion.

At length the volunteers being called out, and furnished with ammunition, commenced a brisk fire upon the assailants, and drove them to their quarters: after which the captain of the volunteers left a strong piquet to watch and guard their town. All the soldiers in the barracks were entirely ignorant of what had taken place, except the parties concerned in the outrage. In the morning the police officers were sent to the barracks, to discover the offenders: the commanding officer gave them all the assistance in his power; and the result was, that a captain, two lieutenants, and a sergeant, were taken and lodged in Horsham gaol: after a few days, however, the officers were admitted to bail, but the sergeant remained in confinement.

In the month of February, 1811, having received a route for Lewes, we marched by the way of Shoreham and Brighton, and arriving at Lewes, were quartered in the barracks at the west end of the town.

About this time liberty being given to the militia to volunteer into the regular army, we made several attempts to get our regiment filled up, by sending officers to the different militia regiments to recruit for us. My master went to Portsmouth, but met with little or no success; for as the militia there had some idea that we were on the eve of going to Spain and Portugal, the major returned without a single volunteer.

One day we had a particular parade, with the locks of our muskets in our hands; all the officers' servants were ordered to attend: my lock not being over clean, the major, to show his impartiality, ordered me three days' drill, but the next day, being Saturday, I took care to whiten the windows a little before drill time; when the bugle sounded I left them as they were, and ran for my musket: the major met me as I was coming out of the kitchen, and ordered me back: so that by these means I got clear of the thing I so much detested.

The regiment had now completely recovered from the shock which it received in the island of Walcheren; every week recruits joined us from the north of England, and different parts of Scotland and Ireland, also draughts from several militia regiments; so that we were now about eight hundred and fifty strong, most of us from eighteen to thirty years of age.

By this time the regiment had attained to a high state of discipline and military order, and all our arms and accoutrements were in excellent condition. Colonel Johnson was also very strict in the inspection of our necessaries, especially our shoes, shirts, brushes, &c. Every man had, or, should have had, two spare shirts, two pair of good shoes, two pair of stockings or socks, three brushes, one razor and soap box, one screw driver and worm, two pair of gaiters, and one great coat, with several other smaller things.

In short, every preparation was made in order to be ready whenever the government called for our services, which call was expected every day. At length the general commanding the district came to review us; after which he made his report to the war-office that we were fit for actual service, and in a few days, we expected the route. In this we were not disappointed, for on Sunday the 2nd of June, 1811, the route arrived for our march to, and embarkation at, Portsmouth, with as little delay as possible.

My master having lost his right arm at Flushing, was appointed to command the regimental depot, and I expected to remain with him:

indeed, he told me he would keep me if possible; so that I confidently expected to stay in England: but the major failed in his endeavours to retain me. Being young and healthy, and fit for service, the colonel insisted that I should go to Spain and Portugal, so that no arguments produced by the major in my favour could turn the colonel from his purpose, and I was ultimately compelled to go with the regiment.

In the evening my master told me what had passed between himself and the colonel: "but," said he, "if you return to England, I will have you again." On the 3rd, Mr. Risdale the surgeon, and Lieut. M'Kay, were invited to our house, to take a parting glass with the major, who gave me an excellent character to these gentlemen, saying, he had never been better suited in his life. He also gave orders to these officers, that if I should be in need of money whilst in the peninsula, they were to let me have it, and place it to his account. When I went into the major's room, "Now, Green," said he, "if there is anything in my house which you need, you may have it with pleasure." He urged me to take a shirt or two: I refused, saying, I was obliged to him for his goodness. He then gave me twenty shillings to buy tea, sugar, or anything else that I might want for the voyage; again promising, should I return, he would be my friend.

After finishing my work, and bidding my mistress farewell, I left the room, with a heart as full as possible, and retired into the kitchen in the greatest sorrow of mind. The major followed me, and taking me by the hand in a most affectionate manner, consoled me. We then parted; and so completely was I overcome by the major's kindness that I was bathed in tears: he was himself much affected, having something to do to keep down his feelings. Indeed, the kindness of Major Thompson was very great, and I shall ever remember him with grateful respect. I retired to rest with these uncomfortable feelings, but was aroused at half-past three o clock by the sound of the bugle. I arose immediately, and, after adjusting my knapsack, joined my company, when the regiment moved off towards Brighton.

CHAPTER 7

March to Portsmouth

The first day we marched to Shoreham: it being the king's birthday, there was great rejoicing in several towns through which we passed; but I could not help reflecting that many of us were marching to our death-day. The next day we arrived at Arundel, the town at which we had the affray with the inhabitants, but no disturbance took place on the occasion. On the 7th we reached the city of Chichester, and on the 8th arrived at Portsmouth, marched down to the point, and embarked without having a moment's liberty to leave the ranks; which seemed hard, as we wanted several necessaries for the voyage.

Nothing happened worth notice until the 18th June, when we weighed anchor, and set sail for Portugal: about three o'clock in the afternoon we passed the Needles, and got into the British Channel. The Needles, so called, is a very narrow passage of the sea between the Isle of Wight and Hampshire: so narrow is the passage, and so high some of the rocks, that to a stranger it appears dangerous. We sailed along the coast of Dorsetshire, Devonshire, and Cornwall, until the 21st June, when we altered our course southwest by south, and soon reached the Bay of Biscay, which we knew by the mighty swell of its waters, for the waves were so large that the ships disappeared for several seconds of time together, and then rose to the summit of the waves with all the majesty and grandeur imaginable: no persons can conceive the awful effect without they saw it.

Our vessel, the *Amphitrite*, stood it very well: we had a good stiff breeze of favourable wind, so that we glided along the trackless deep, though, by the bye, many of us were very sick; for when the vessel had gained the summit of the wave, down she went as though she would not have stopped until she had reached the bottom, up she started, and then rolled and staggered along.

On the 25th we came in sight of the north-west point of Spain, called Cape Finisterre. We now began to think of our army in that country, especially as we were about joining them.

We continued our course until the 27th, on the morning of which we discovered the rocks of Lisbon, a few leagues ahead. About ten o'clock, a smart breeze springing up, and receiving a pilot on board, we were wafted into the Tagus, one of the finest rivers in Europe. We passed Belem, the key fort of this river, and sailed until we reached that part of the river opposite the Black-Horse Square, where we dropped anchor in deep water, and within pistol-shot of Lisbon, the capital of the kingdom of Portugal. This is a very commodious harbour, large enough to contain several hundreds of ships of any burden; indeed, at this period, one of our three-deckers lay within one hundred yards of the shore.

28th. This morning we landed, and marched to St. Domingo Convent, the habitation of monks and friars: it was spacious, and divided into small apartments; we had neither beds nor blankets, having to lie on the convent floor in our great coats. These were our first quarters: although indifferent, they were palaces, compared with what we had in different parts of these kingdoms.

The city of Lisbon is situated on the north bank of the Tagus; the old city, which was swallowed up by an earthquake in the year 1755, stood on the south or opposite bank of this river. At present there are several houses, and some traffic carried on there; but it is nothing to New Lisbon, which reaches about three miles in length and nearly two in breadth in the broadest part. It contains some very handsome houses, squares, and churches, some of which are decorated with images of gold and silver, wrought with precious stones. Whilst at this place I saw the procession of the Host; the people in all directions took off their hats, but others that were more pious went down, on their knees. On one occasion I neglected to take off my cap, which was noticed by one of the peasants, who accosted me with "*Ah! bruta! Ah! bruta!*" meaning, in English, that I was a brute.

Whilst in these countries, I have often known some of the Roman Catholics, while counting their beads in the evening, and repeating certain prayers and *Ave-Marias*, if any little thing put them out of their way during these exercises, they would rise up in the greatest passion, cursing and swearing, and using other improper language; which looked worse, in my view, than the mere nominal Christian of England; for few indeed, however bad, would curse and pray with the same breath. But what astonished me the most, was, that these people, who were ever boasting of the sanctity of their religion, should pay so little regard to the sabbath, more than going to mass, &c.

But to return. There are in this city two streets nearly eight hundred yards long; one of them is occupied chiefly by goldsmiths, the other by silversmiths and those who are employed in grinding diamonds and other precious stones to fix into rings, crucifixes, and other ornaments. There is also in one of the squares a large and beautiful statue, the eyes of which were, as I have been informed, valued at from two to three millions sterling: they were two diamonds of a prodigious size: the Portuguese offered a very great sum to the French not to molest them; but they took the money, and the eyes too, and would have taken the beautiful statue, which was solid copper, but something or other prevented them.

We remained at Lisbon only seven days, having received a route to join Lord Wellington, then lying in the province of Estremadura, near the fortified town of Elvas. On the morning of the 5th July, we formed in order to march, and moved off right in front through the city to the quay side, where the regiment was embarked on board a number of transport boats, which were to carry us up the river as far as a small village called Villada. We had sails to the boats, but it being a calm, we were forced to take to the oars. In the boat to which I belonged I accidentally met with a man named Parker, who also came from Louth: no person can imagine how pleased I was with the man, because he was a fellow-countryman; but I could not understand at that time to what family of the Parker's he belonged; I know very well now, and have since heard that the poor fellow was drowned while engaged in the transport service.

We sailed very pleasantly up the Tagus for about fourteen miles: we then got into a wrong current, and were carried into a creek, and the current running, strong, we were completely stranded on the south bank of the Tagus, but received no damage whatever; only being delayed till the tide served the next morning. Although this was but the 5th of July, the harvest was not only reaped, but the corn nearly all thrashed out, and fit for the market. I was considerably alarmed during the night by the croaking of frogs, which was nearly as loud as the quacking of ducks: I was filled with the thoughts of rattlesnakes, and other noxious reptiles, but found nothing of the sort to hurt me.

In the morning at three o'clock the tide began to flow; we with great difficulty launched our boat, and got out of the creek, steered full east, or towards the rising sun, and arrived in safety at Villada at eleven o'clock p. m., where our colonel had provided half a pint of port wine a man. Having partaken of this refreshment, and rested about an hour, we commenced our march in this hot climate, with heavy load on our backs, and not being accustomed to such fatigue, it went very hard with us for several days; but after a severe march of sixteen miles, we arrived at Santarem, at five o'clock in the evening, and took up our quarters in a large convent in the high town, which is beautifully situated on the north bank of the Tagus.

It is a place of some trade, and has a good market: the population may be about five or six thousand. I have been informed that there are no less than fourteen convents in this place, beside several churches; consequently, a great number of monks and friars, many of whom are maintained by the poor peasants: they wear a coarse coat or cloak, tied round them with a rope, at the ends of which are several knots tied according to the order to which they belong.

But to return: on the 8th of July, after recovering three days' bread and meat, three pints of wine, and sixty rounds of ammunition, we commenced our movements towards Golegain: with this load on our backs, altogether amounting to little short of four stones weight—the hardships we endured from this, and the change of climate and provision, together with the abundance of fruit, and drinking cold water when exceedingly hot, our men began to be taken with fevers and fluxes.

We have sent from ten to twenty in a day to the general hospital, where many of them died, and others continued a long time. We reached Golegain about eleven o'clock, and took up our quarters in the miserable and wretched houses of the inhabitants, a description of which will be found in the course of this narrative.

9th. We marched to Punheta, distant about fourteen miles: this little town attracted my notice so much, that I must mention a few particulars concerning it. It is situated on the north bank of the Tagus, an arm of which runs through the village: the inhabitants have a bridge over it made of boats, moored at a certain distance from each other: spars are thrown from one boat to another, and planked right across. Waggons and carts may pass over with the greatest safety, but every man on horseback must dismount and lead his horse over for fear of accident.

10th. The bugle sounded at the usual hour, namely three o'clock, when we moved off left in front; that is, the left wing taking the lead.

There is a certain advantage on the line of march to those that go first, whether in a regiment, brigade, or a division. In order to give each the advantage in turn, the right of the regiment, brigade, or division, went first one day, and the left the next, unless it was at a time when we were near the enemy, and in expectation of an engagement: we then went according to circumstances. This day we marched very regularly, and kept our ranks; for the distance was only ten miles.

We arrived at Abrantes at seven o'clock, the right wing was quartered in the city, the left crossed the Tagus, and encamped close by the side of this delightful river. This city is very strong both by nature and by art: it stands on a very high hill, which commands the surrounding country in every direction but one, in which it is strongly guarded by a fort. There are a number of criminals constantly employed at the public works of this place. Every morning, when going to their employment, they were marched out of prison, chained together two, and two.

Death would have been preferable to the, poor wretched beings; for when they had done their work, which they were compelled to do like galley slaves, they were shut up in a dark and loathsome prison, having nothing to comfort themselves with but a little coarse bread and water: indeed, the prisons in Portugal are most wretched places. Here we received beautiful white bread instead of biscuit, and good wine instead of rum.

On the 11th we halted, and washed our clothes, which needed this necessary operation. The next morning, we recommenced our route with the usual load of three days' provisions on our shoulders; and crossing the bridge of boats, which reached nearly two hundred yards, marched along a tedious road through a wilderness, scarcely meeting with one solitary village for thirty-two miles; which may be attributed to our having taken a wrong road, and marched fourteen miles about. Oh! what a day was this; parched with thirst, and exposed to the scorching rays of the sun, which greatly distressed us. However, in the evening we reached Gaveon.

Our baggage not arriving, we were under the necessity of halting the next day in the miserable village of Gaveon, the inhabitants of which were wretched in the extreme: their houses were not so good as our stable, some indeed not better than a hog-sty. Several of the children were nearly naked; women barefooted, and almost starved, to death for want of food; besides being almost lost with vermin.

On the morning of the 14th, our baggage and provisions having joined us, and having received our biscuit, we moved off at three o'clock to a small dirty village called Gafere, and were quartered on the wretched peasantry, some of whom were entirely naked. How happy the people of England, when compared with the wretched inhabitants of Portugal!

15th. The bugle sounded at the usual time, and after forming, we moved off to Portalegre, distant about fourteen miles, and took up our quarters in a convent at the gate leading to Elvas. Portalegre is a very good-looking town for this country, having several convents and churches, and one of the handsomest chapels in the kingdom, decorated with all the trappings of Popery, such as having the images dressed in the most gaudy manner. There is also in the market-place one of the most beautiful fountains of water I ever beheld: the weather being very hot, we were constant visitors to this beautiful piece of sculpture. There are several productions of this sort in the peninsula. Here we halted only one day. This place is walled round, but not being fortified, is not sufficiently strong to withstand an enemy: the inhabitants were miserably poor,

Early in the morning of the 17th we marched to Aronches, and reached there, at eleven o'clock; crossed the river, and encamped in a wood opposite the town. The appearance of this place is very gothic: it stands on a high hill, completely surrounded by a wall, on the top of which are several towers. At the bottom of the hill runs murmuring along a beautiful shallow river. Aronches is about four leagues from the city of Elvas (I had a relation died in the hospital of that place, called Samuel Ashton) and only five leagues from Badajoz, the grave of Englishmen.

We remained here until the 21st, when the army broke up from this part of Spain, and moved off in the direction of Ciudad Rodrigo. We joined the 7th Division, then consisting of the following regiments: the 51st, 85th, the Chasseurs Britanniques, three regiments of the German Legion Light Infantry, three Portuguese regiments, and a brigade of Flying Artillery, commanded by Major-General Houston.

We marched from Aronches to Nisa in three days. Nisa is a smart little town, surrounded by a wall, having several churches, a convent, and a good market We halted in this place until the 31st of July; and then marched in the direction of Castel Branco. First day we crossed the Tagus at Villa Velha; in crossing this river we had the most romantic views; high towering mountains, and rough craggy rocks, together with the swiftly-gliding stream of the Tagus, making it altogether a scene highly interesting. When we came to the bridge, which was made of boats, similar to the bridge at Punheta and Abrantes, the whole of the divisions crossed over; but the bridge sprung very much, and care was taken of the horses, for fear of accidents.

On the other side, on the top of the hill, stands a wretched look-ing village, called Villa Velha, from which the pass takes its name: here we encamped for the night. The next day we reached Cernada, which is pleasantly situated, having cultivated fields around it, which is not always the case in these parts. The third day we reached the city of Castel Branco, which is a very healthy place, having several springs and fountains of good water. Here is also the palace of a bishop, and sev-eral nobles reside in this town and neighbourhood: there is also a very handsome cathedral church, and several other churches and chapels; and an old castle, from which the town takes its name; We had also a general hospital, with a depot of convalescent soldiers, and a magazine of military stores and provisions for the army. The market of this place is well supplied.

On the 4th we reached a pretty little village called St. Miguel; on the 5th, Pedrogos, and on the 6th, we arrived at Pena Macor, a large town situated on the top of a ridge of hills; having a castle and several churches and convents. The inhabitants. of this part of Portugal are very polite; for when a peasant met a soldier, he would bow with the greatest respect, I also have remarked, that when the poorest peasants meet on the road, they will bow and salute each other with "*Viva, Senor,*" or some other kind word,

August 7th. We moved off in front, marched, over high mountains, and through, valleys covered with brushwood and bushes so high that the army was frequently hid from the view of each other. We arrived at Sabugal, and encamped under the chestnut trees about half a mile from the town. Sabugal has the appearance of ancient grandeur, being surrounded by a gothic wall, and having a castle, the walls of which are in good condition; but the town is small, not containing more than six hundred people.

8th. We marched to Alfaites, a pleasant village near the Spanish frontier; and on the 9th arrived at Villa Major, a frontier village of Portugal, only two miles from Spain, and remained there until Sep-tember 22nd. Villa Major is a neat village, consisting of about thirty houses, and one hundred and twenty inhabitants. It has one church, two chapels, and a small market; and a river runs through it, which makes it delightfully pleasant. Wood was plentiful and within a short distance, mulberries, grapes, and figs were in abundance.

Our company and three others, were quartered in the church. During our stay here, I saw the Roman Catholics bury some of their dead according to the superstitions of the church of Rome. Previous to the arrival of our regiment in this place, I had a very severe attack of fever and flux. I was left at Nisa, where I remained about three weeks: in consequence of leaving Nisa, before I was well, the fever fell into my feet and ankles, making me a complete cripple; in which state I remained for several weeks, not being able to do my duty.

While in this church, we experienced a most awful thunderstorm, the claps of thunder being the loudest and most terrible I ever heard; during which the rain fell in torrents, and the wind blowing a complete hurricane, greatly alarmed us. I have no doubt but it appeared worse to us than it really was, on account of the echo of the church.

September 22nd. In consequence of some hostile movements of the enemy, who was only six leagues from this place, we received orders to occupy a small village called Aldea Dabeira, only three miles distant: we stayed there until the 24th, and then marched to Guinaldo, which was only three leagues from Ciudad Rodrigo, a strong garrison in possession of the French Army. Our regiment remained here until the 27th, when the enemy advancing from Salamanca in great force, compelled us to retreat and take up a strong position near Sabugal, where we had a little skirmishing, but nothing of any consequence; that was reserved for some future period.

The season being far advanced, and winter coming on, we broke up from before Sabugal, and went into cantonments, or winter quarters; the 7th Division at Pena Macor, the light division on the frontiers of Portugal, the 5th Division at the city of Guarda, and the other divisions so arranged that we could have been collected in a few days. Our regiment lay at Pena Macor fourteen days, and then went to Pedrogos, a small village on the Castel Branco road, distant two leagues. When the retreat began, in consequence of my lameness, I, with several other sick men of different regiments, was sent to the general hospital at Celerico; however I soon joined the army again, having recovered the strength of my ankles, but not by applying liniments, for I rubbed several bottles of mixture into them, but was no better. Being advised by an old soldier to go to a fountain, and let the water run upon them,

I did so, and soon recovered my strength; and a party of the 68th coming through this place, I joined them, and started for Pedrogos.

On this journey I passed through the city of Guarda, which is situated on a lofty mountain, the ascent thereto being four miles. The distance to the city is increased by the zig-zag way in which the roads are necessarily cut, or no carriage could ever travel up those lofty hills. The city is very handsome and compact, being built chiefly of stone: there are convents, churches, and public buildings in abundance, from the top of which we had a view for sixty or seventy miles, or perhaps more.

On this march also I passed through a village called Val de Lobos, the meaning of which, in English, is the valley of wolves. There are a great number of these animals in this part of Portugal, but they seldom attack a person in the day time, although they are terrible in the night. A man of our army having to go a journey by night, was attacked by them and devoured, nothing but his bones being found. I saw a mule at Freynada, which had its thigh so mangled with a wolf, that it was with difficulty healed. During my stay in this country, I saw several, but passed through the valley of wolves without ever seeing an animal of this sort; and arrived in good health at Pedrogos, with about eight hundred new flannel shirts for the regiment: the shirts were full sized, with long sleeves, which I have no doubt had a tendency to preserve health more than linen shirts could do.

Pedrogos is a pleasant village, having plenty of wood and good water within half a mile of the town, so that we were well situated for the winter, which is very cold and rainy, but scarcely any frost or snow, except on the mountains, where it lies all the year. In this place we received our provisions regularly: our daily allowance was as follows: one pound of beef, one pound of biscuit or one pound and a half of bread, one-third of a pint of rum, and two ounces of rice. Our beef was better than I had ever seen it before, for there was good pasture and rest for the cattle, which gave them time to fatten. Very frequently in the summer season, when we had been some time on the march, our meat was literally like carrion; and if twenty pounds had been offered for a small quantity of suet, it would have been impossible to obtain it.

CHAPTER 8

The Army Invests Ciudad Rodrigo

While we lay at Pedrogos, General Castanos, with his baggage and suite, passed through on his way to the Spanish frontier. There was nothing remarkable in his appearance; in person he was below the middle stature. I and several others were placed as a guard of honour to receive this celebrated Spanish hero: the guard was drawn up in the market-place, and waited nearly two hours for him: at length he arrived, and we presented arms and conducted him to the quarters of the commanding officer, who invited him to partake of refreshment; but he politely refused, and passed through, without alighting from his carriage.

While at this place, I mounted guard: during the day we received as prisoners two Portuguese peasants, who had been employed in the commissary department, having in charge several fine bullocks for the army: but these two rascals had contrived to exchange some of the fattest and best for some that were not half so-good; thereby making to themselves a deal of money by their villainy. In the night I went on sentry to guard these two Portuguese thieves: with my bayonet in my hand, I examined the prisoners, for we had several of our own men in the guardroom, but all was right.

In the course of half an hour, however, one of the Portuguese prisoners contrived to get to the tiles, the place, not being underdrawn; and it being extremely dark, he succeeded in breaking through; but the sergeant and some of the men running round to the back of the guardroom, luckily caught the gentleman as he was falling from the tiles, and brought him back to his prison, when I trimmed him well for his want of civility, in departing without my leave; for had he made his escape, I most probably should have suffered for it. However, he remained as quiet as possible until the morning, when we sent them both off under a strong escort to Pena Macor, the headquarters of the division; and what became of them I never heard.

In this place we had one parade every morning properly dressed, and one fatigue parade in the afternoon, to cut wood and bring it home to our quarters; but we were prohibited from cutting fruit and olive trees, of which there was a great number. Here is an oil press, where the olive oil is made in its purest form. I was very fond of it, and have often had a cup full put into a new loaf: it is a good substitute for butter, and tastes very well. The inhabitants use a great deal of it in their soaps, &c. and it answers the place of flesh meat to many families in these parts: it has no unpleasant taste whatever. Beef fried in this oil adds greatly to its flavour, makes it more palatable, and I believe more wholesome—We remained here very quietly and comfortably, though we had neither beds nor bedding, having to lay on the bare floors of the houses, until the beginning of January, when it began to be whispered we were soon to move from this peaceable place; and there was something like truth in these reports, for on the 9th January 1812 an order came for the regiment to join the division at Pena Macor.

On the 10th, according to order, we marched to Pena Macor, and joined the 7th Division; and on the 11th crossed the wilderness, which I have mentioned before, and arrived at Sabugal: on the 12th we reached Alfaites; on the 13th Guinaldo, where we remained a short time, having very strong guards and piquets, not being more than sixteen miles from Ciudad Rodrigo; for at this time the army was forming for the purpose of storming this fortification. It appears that it was absolutely necessary to get possession of Ciudad Rodrigo and Badajoz before any good could be done in these parts; for the enemy, having strong garrisons, and plenty of provisions and ammunition, could have annoyed us very much and if we had advanced without reducing them, we should have been forced either to have left an army to watch and keep them in awe, or subjected ourselves to their repeated attacks; our supplies would have been cut off, or we might have been left without provisions and ammunition.

The army having now collected, was actively employed night and day, from the 13th, in order to complete the works, which were no sooner done, than our batteries opened upon the town with tremendous fury, and continued to play until they made several practicable breaches in the walls, the army that invested the place only waited the signal to storm.

On the evening of the 19th the troops employed formed in five columns, and waited to commence the work of death. General Pack's brigade was ordered to advance, and to make a false attempt at the breaches; but such was the courage of this brave general and his men, that it was turned into reality: and the advanced guard, under the command of Major Lynch, took possession of the enemy's outwork, taking several prisoners. The main breach was stormed by the second battalion of the Fifth Regiment, led on by Major Ridge. The enemy stood to their posts, and fought with determination, contesting every inch; nor did they surrender, until our brave soldiers had completely established themselves in the streets of the town, when all further resistance was evidently unavailing.

The loss of our army, from the commencement to the conclusion of this brilliant affair, was about twelve hundred in killed and wounded. Major-General Mackinnon was blown up, and the commander of the light division received a wound, of which he died on the 24th January. This action was short, pointed, and carried on with vigour on both sides. The loss of the enemy in killed was great: we took one thousand seven hundred prisoners, one hundred and fifty-three pieces of cannon, and an immense quantity of ammunition and stores.

Although our regiment was not engaged at this place, but was employed in covering the besieging army; yet all were entitled to the honour, for, if called upon, they would have entered the breaches and stormed the city, with as much resolution and valour as those who had been employed.

As soon as things in Ciudad Rodrigo were settled, Lord Wellington made preparations, with as little delay as possible, for the siege of Badajoz. About this time, I was taken very ill of a fever, to which we were very subject in this climate, in consequence of our fatigues. I lay several days in a village on the Castel Branco road; indeed I was so exceedingly ill that I was taken in a waggon belonging to the royal waggon train, and carried to the general hospital at the latter place, where I continued ill several weeks. I at length recovered a little, and got out of the hospital, but was so weak that I could scarcely walk: yet I had to do the duty of the depot. An officer of our regiment, at Castel Branco, took me from the depot to be his groom: I went with him to his quarters, and remained a few days, having nothing to do but to groom an ass, and tent him while grazing. I was again taken ill, and sent to the hospital.

The general doctor no sooner saw me than he swore he would have me ducked in a tub of water, because I had left the other hospital too soon, but he was better to me than I expected, using me very well during my stay under his care. While I was in this hospital, which was close by the road side, our gallant army marched through on their way to Badajoz. I shall mention a few particulars concerning their march, although I was not with them. The day after the regiment left this place, they went to Cernada; the second day they reached Villa Velha; the third day, Nisa; on the sixth Oronches, and from thence, on the seventh, to Estremos, where they lay until things were in readiness to commence the siege of Badajoz.

I shall now leave them, and relate the sufferings through which I passed. I now began to recover, got out of the hospital, and joined the depot, where I remained about fourteen days. A day being appointed to select out of the convalescent soldiers those who were fit for the army, I thought, if it were possible, I would go and join my regiment, for I abominably detested my present situation and employment, having to clean the streets of the dirty Portuguese every morning before breakfast; for we were obliged to take all the dirt away that the inhabitants made, and that was not a little.

They are the dirtiest people in this place I ever saw, for almost all the men, women, and children deposit filth of every kind in the streets, old houses, or in back lanes; and all this we had to clean away for our own sakes and that of our officers. If we were not ill, this was enough to make us so. The morning came that we were to be picked out to join the army: at this time, I was unfit for service, and my looks were against me. I was placed on the left of the rear rank, and, in order that I might pass the better, I had prepared a piece of coarse woollen cloth, with which I rubbed my face to make the colour come, and this I continued to do until the doctor and commanding officer came up to me: I passed their inspection very well, and was ordered to march the next morning to join my regiment. No man could have been more delighted than I was at the thoughts of leaving this place.

The next morning, we formed in marching order, and waited the word of command; but I was taken so ill on the parade, that I could hardly stand in the ranks. However, the word "march" was given, and we moved off; but I could not keep up with the division. My old companion, James Mann, remained with me, and we followed as fast as my strength would permit, but it was with the greatest difficulty that I reached Cernada, which was only twelve miles. The next morning my condition was deplorable, having nowhere to rest myself but on the bare floor of an uninhabited house, unable to lift up my head, and having no sort of food that I could partake of; indeed, if I had had luxuries, I could not have tasted them. The following morning, I started for Villa Velha, but only reached a small village three miles off, and was some hours performing even that journey; for had not my friend James been with me, I must have perished from the want of assistance.

We remained in this village two or three days, and were so distressed, that I thought it was all over with me. A part of the army passing through, a doctor was brought to my assistance, who ordered me some medicine, but by some means or other it was neglected, and I was still left in this sad and wretched condition, without money, medicine, or one single comfort in my possession. Here I lay in a Portuguese village, the inhabitants of which could not render me any assistance; and none but those who have gone through such trials, can tell what I suffered at this period.

At length it came to this crisis, that I must either die in this distressed town, or make an effort to get to Nisa. For this purpose, we started; but how or in what manner I got to Villa Velha, which was only four miles, I know not, having to carry a load something more than three stones weight, and being in a high fever, which frequently deprived me of my recollection, so that I knew not where I was, or what I was doing. However, we reached Villa Velha, and took up our quarters in a house by the roadside: James made me a kind of bed, obtained a little coffee, and provided for me in the best manner possible. The army was now moving rapidly upon Badajoz; the last division arriving encamped near the bridge.

The next morning they were put in motion: James then applied to the general doctor, who came to examine me; but the moment he saw me, and had felt my pulse, he flew into a violent rage, swearing he would have me flogged: the moment the provost marshal came up, he called me everything he pleased; and there I stood before him unmoved by his threats, and unable to make a defence for myself; and all this scolding was because I had left the hospital at Castel Branco before I was well, and indeed I had nearly paid the forfeit of my life for my rashness, for I had no business whatever to march in this condition. But the doctor's words were only like the wind, for, instead of punishing me, he ordered a mule to carry me to Nisa, which was a distance of nine miles.

I with difficulty got my clothes on, was put on the mule's back, and started to Nisa; but of all the men I ever saw, the Spanish muleteer who accompanied me was the most unfeeling; for he drove his mule before the rest, making the poor animal trot all the way; and if the mule slackened its pace, he would run at and kick it on the legs and hams, crying, in the Spanish language, "cursed, cursed;" this was because he had a sick soldier to carry. I begged he would let the mule go its own pace, but to no purpose. I really believe I should have shot the rascal, had I been able; for no one can conceive what I suffered while with this inhuman wretch. However, I got to Nisa, and made known to the Portuguese what the Spaniard had done unto me; and when they heard it, some of them were about to thrash him for his unfeeling conduct.

I remained in the market-place until my comrade arrived: he then took me into a house, in which I, lay for seven days in a state of insensibility. In this place I could have anything I fancied, for my comrade was connected with certain men who knew how to raise the wind: I was entirely ignorant at the time how it was done, but I learned afterwards that it was by making false returns, and drawing provisions for a certain number of men, when no such men were to be found: I have known them to have provisions and wine in abundance.

After remaining in this place seven days, the sick men were ordered for Abrantes General Hospital. I should have mentioned that an officer, of the name of Coxon, a native of the neighbourhood of Louth, was commanding officer here: he is since dead, and his widow is now (1827), residing at Louth.

A great number of sick men were left in this place. On the day of our departure, every man was provided with an ass, and a proper supply of provisions for the journey: we then started for Abrantes, each man being mounted upon his donkey. I had a very good one, but did not keep him all the journey; for we had only proceeded two miles from Nisa, when we came to a river, which is fordable in summer and in dry weather, but there having been a great fall of rain, it was swollen into a formidable stream. Most of the asses swam over with the men on their backs; but a number of stones, five or six feet high, being placed just one pace from each other, for a passage for the peasantry, I, rather than have my clothes wet, attempted to cross by them.

I accordingly sent my ass into the river, with my knapsack, &c., and then began to cross the stones; but when I had got three-fourths of the way over, into the river I went, and had it not been for the kindness of a man behind me, the current would have carried me down, but he caught hold of my coat, and most probably saved me from a watery grave. When I got to the other side, I found that my ass, knapsack, and everything belonging to me, were gone: but there being an old ass left instead of my own, with difficulty I got upon its back, and rode the remainder of the journey, which was two leagues, in my wet clothes, and had to lay all night on a cold marl floor.

Anyone would think that this would have sent me to my long home, but, strange as it may appear, from that day I began to recover. The next morning, I found my knapsack, and then started for Gaveon, and reached it about noon. This day my fever left me, my appetite returned, and I have reason to be thankful that I never had a fever after, but was always able to do my duty until the 31st August 1813. The next day we arrived at Abrantes, and were admitted into the general hospital, where I remained three weeks; having recovered my strength, I left the hospital, joined the depot, and did my duty.

While in this place, I and my comrade got some new shirts and shoes, on purpose to sell, to raise a little money, being uncommonly destitute: he sold his first: the next day an order was given for an inspection of necessaries, and every man that could not produce his new things was flogged; so that my poor comrade was not only confined, but actually received two or three dozen lashes for his conduct. I took care, however, not to offer mine for sale until the first day's march, when we were under no control.

We left Abrantes, and joined the 68th Regiment, not missing one single skirmish by having been sick and absent, but joined in full time to take our part against the common enemy of Europe. Our regiment lay a few days at Estremos, and then marched in the direction of the enemy, who it was expected would make a desperate effort to save Badajoz from falling into our hands. The seventh Division, with two other divisions of infantry, and two brigades of cavalry, under the command of Lieutenant-General Graham, moved in the direction of Valverde; and General Hill, with a considerable force under him, moved off in another direction: by these movements we covered the besieging army of Badajoz, so that it was next to an impossibility for the enemy to raise the siege without bringing either General Hill or General Graham to an engagement: but nothing of importance took place with our division of the British Army.

Badajoz was invested in the middle of March: the troops employed at this important siege were the third, fourth, and light divisions. Whilst part of this force was occupied in building batteries and throwing up the works, the enemy made a sortie, with about two thousand men. Their design was either to destroy the works, or retard their progress;

but in this they were unsuccessful; and notwithstanding the fury with which they advanced upon our working parties, they were driven back into Badajoz with great loss.

On the 25th March the first battery was opened within two hundred yards of the walls of the town, and on the same night a fort was taken by storm. It was defended by two hundred and fifty men; and five hundred of our brave men, consisting of detachments from different regiments, rushed into it, and took it at the point of the bayonet. The three commanding officers of these little detachments were wounded; a brigade major was the only officer killed. The enemy defending the fort were for the most part put to the sword. About this time the weather was very wet and bad, which greatly distressed our troops.

On the 6th April three breaches were considered practicable, and Lord Wellington was determined to lose no time, but to commence the assault that very night. Accordingly, the troops destined for this important service were collected at eight o'clock, without knapsack; and about ten this awful conflict took place; General Picton's division commencing the attack on the castle of Badajoz, having been provided with a number of ladders for that purpose.

The men were led on to this noble enterprise by Major-General Kempt, who received a wound at the beginning of the storm: the soldiers were not at all discouraged by this catastrophe, but continued their vigorous efforts until they had completely succeeded in taking the castle. But the 4th and light divisions met with such a formidable resistance, and obstacles so numerous, that they could not establish themselves within the place, but were drawn off from that part of the action at twelve o'clock at night, after losing a great number of officers and men.

But the intended false attack, under Lieutenant-General Leith, was completely successful: the brave men engaged in this part of the work, turned an outwork, gained the ditch, and climbing upon the ramparts, took possession of a part of the town. Having obtained possession of the castle and town, the governor and his staff were necessitated to take shelter. in the fort of St. Christoval, which they surrendered on the 7th April. The French garrison of Badajoz consisted of five thousand men, twelve hundred of whom were killed or wounded during the operations, beside what were lost during the storming of the castle, breaches, &c., which must have been two thousand or more.

The total loss of our army, together with the Portuguese, in this bloody siege and assault, from the commencement of the operations to the surrender, was seventy-two officers, fifty-three sergeants, two drummers, and nine hundred and ten privates killed; three hundred and six officers, two hundred and sixteen sergeants, seventeen drummers, and three thousand two hundred and forty-eight privates wounded; one sergeant and sixty-eight privates missing: making in all four thousand eight hundred and ninety-one killed, wounded, and missing: so that altogether we lost in this place, in both sieges, perhaps more than six thousand men.

The conduct of the British troops during this hazardous and eventful service was above all praise; indeed, Lord Wellington himself observed, that he was unable to express the sense which he entertained of the gallantry of both officers and men.

The city of Badajoz is about the size of Boston, in this county; but it would be difficult to ascertain the population, as the towns in Spain and Portugal have so many convents and churches, which make them appear larger than they really are.

During the siege and investment of Badajoz, and the operation of the British arms in this part of the Peninsula, the French Army of Salamanca made a sudden dash into Portugal, no doubt to draw our attention from our principal object. The enemy advanced by the way of Sabugal and Pedrogos to Castel Branco, forcing our depot of sick and convalescent soldiers at the last-mentioned place to escape to Nisa. The Portuguese peasants fled to the mountains in the greatest confusion. The enemy reached Cernada; but as soon as the French general heard of the fate of Badajoz; he retreated in the greatest haste: the cavalry, however, under Sir Stapleton Cotton overtook his rearguard, brought them to action, and compelled them to fly in confusion, with a considerable loss in killed and wounded; and one hundred and fifty prisoners fell into our hands.

Our division was now ordered into cantonments at Castel Branco, where we lay until the 4th of June; but the greater part of the army advanced to the Spanish frontiers, and to the frontiers of Portugal, A part of the town was allotted to our brigade, and three small streets to our regiment. I was quartered at the house of an old widow. We had one parade every day in the large square at eleven o'clock in the morning, and a roll-call in the evening at five. In the house where I was quartered the old woman had a large image of St. Louis, which had lost a hand.

One afternoon I repaired the image by fastening on the hand, which pleased her so much, that I became a great favourite with her. I did not, however, continue in her good graces long; for in consequence of some trifling error in my conduct, she ran after me with a hatchet to knock me on the head.

While at this place, numbers of our sick men joined us, and we had considerably improved after our late fatiguing marches, both in strength and appearance, having had our shoes and clothes properly repaired. Provisions, ammunition, and stores were sent up the country in abundance, and the battering train was brought up to the frontiers. In short, all the time of this cessation was occupied in preparing for an advance into the heart of Spain; for having possession of all the fortified places on the frontiers of both kingdoms, nothing now prevented us from entering into that country.

While in Portugal and Spain, we were distressed for the want of money: all the time we had been in that country we never obtained a settlement, neither had we received our clothing from Christmas 1810 up to the present period. The army was often short of salt, soap, needles, and threads although these things were simple, yet they were essential; and to be without them caused us much trouble and uneasiness. I frequently visited the old castle at this place, which stands on a very high hill, and may be seen at the distance of fifty miles: the walls are very thick, but in a ruinous condition.

Chapter 9

Campaign of 1812

By the 3rd of June everything was ready, and on the 4th, we marched towards the frontiers, anticipating that this campaign would produce something decisive and important. On the 5th we marched to Pedrogos, twenty-two miles; and on the 6th to Sabugal, and encamped about half a mile from the town. This day's march was twenty-two miles, through a wild country full of woods and thickets. On the 7th the division halted, and found several French spies in the camp, one of whom was taken, and, as I have heard, was executed on the spot, his papers having been found in a loaf of bread, the worst place in which they could have been secreted. A number of French spies were frequently in our camps, and we had several in the enemy's camps also; so that the contending armies had information of the movements of each other.

On the 8th we moved off left in front, and about twelve o'clock arrived at Albergaria, distant twenty miles; and the weather being exceedingly hot, the men were very much fatigued. On the 9th we marched, and encamped one league from a town, the name of which I never heard. This evening, orders came that we were to be reviewed by His Excellency the Commander in Chief. On the morning of the 10th, we marched towards a plain nine miles distant, where the whole of the 7th Division, with three regiments of cavalry and one brigade of flying artillery, assembled.

We formed in line, the 51st Regiment on the right of the infantry, the German brigade on the left; and on the right of the whole were the brigades of cavalry and artillery, the whole line extending more than three miles. We waited an hour for His Lordship, who then arrived, attended by the following officers: the Prince of Orange, Marshal Beresford, General Hope, and a great number of *aides-de-camp*. His Lordship and staff rode at full speed to the centre of the division, and there took their stand: the ranks were already open, and the whole of the division gave a general salute from right to left, His Lordship, taking off his hat, and remaining uncovered all the time the bands of the different regiments were playing "God save the King."

He then rode to the right of the division, and passed along the front, and up the rear of both infantry and cavalry. We then formed into open column, and marched past His Lordship and staff, each troop of cavalry and company of infantry saluting as they passed by. We again formed into line, and advanced in this position about four miles, the cavalry following as the reserve. After we had been manoeuvred as long as Lord Wellington thought proper, we broke into columns of regiments, and marched to our respective camp-grounds: the fatigues of this day were very great, continuing about ten hours.

On the 11th we halted. Here I bought some bread of the Spaniards at one shilling per pound. Bread was always dear when the army was collected together: I have known a three-pound loaf sell for one Spanish *dollar* and a half, in English money seven shillings and sixpence. On the 12th we encamped on the side of a hill within three miles of Ciudad Rodrigo: in this place the different divisions of the British Army formed a junction, in order to advance against the enemy. Early in the morning of the 13th, we crossed the Agueda, and marched in the direction of Salamanca: in the course of this march, notwithstanding the vigilance of the provost marshal; we obtained a supply of peas, or what we called green forage.

On the 15th we heard that the enemy was only a few miles before us; and on the 16th we fairly saw them drawn up on some heights in front of Salamanca. We formed, expecting they would make a stand on the heights; but, contrary to our expectation, they moved off after a little skirmishing through the city, and took up a position on the other side, leaving about eight hundred men in some convents and colleges, which they had converted into forts. Our division forded the River Tormes two miles above the city, and encamped within cannon-shot of the walls. While in this camp, we had working parties making a fort of a farmhouse and garden about two miles from our camp-ground; and while we were thus employed, Major-General Clinton's division commenced the siege and bombardment of the forts of Salamanca.

The French General Marmont was determined to raise the siege if possible and on the 20th June took up a position about six miles from Salamanca. In consequence of this movement, the whole of the army under the British commander was put in motion, with the exception of the 6th Division, already employed. Just as orders came for the division to march, our men were going to receive their wine, but was obliged to leave it with the quartermaster, and move off as fast as possible.

We had no sooner reached the top of a rising ground, than we saw the different divisions and brigades taking their position. We halted a moment m two, and made another attempt to serve out the wine, but in vain; for we were ordered forward, and continued to advance until we reached the edge of the plain. We then saw the whole of the French Army encamped about one mile below us, the ground forming a gradual descent. On the left of the British position the cannon had already been playing for two hours: here we determined to stand and fight the enemy. It was now beginning to be dusk; when an order came for the 68th Regiment Light Infantry to descend the hill, and take possession of a small village on the left flank of the enemy. We were to be supported by the Duke of Brunswick's Light Infantry, who were to form a line of communication between us and the 7th Division.

We soon took possession of the village, and found that all the people had fled, except an old woman, who was nearly frantic. I obtained liberty to fall out for a few minutes, and before I had time to join, the column was attacked by a strong body of French infantry. Colonel Johnson ordered one company to the principal entrance of the village, and small detachments to each of the lanes: being thus placed, a most desperate firing commenced, the enemy advancing up the main street in great force. The colonel ordered two companies to the charge; but finding they were not sufficiently strong, he commanded the whole forward.

At this time my right-hand front-rank man, a corporal of Captain Gough's company, was killed on the spot, not giving a single struggle; We charged the enemy to the end of the street, and were so near to them, that the colonel pulled one of the French soldiers into our column. It now became so dark that we could scarcely see each other.

The companies that were stationed at the end of the streets were sharply engaged, and my comrades now began to fall in all directions: at length an *aide-de-camp* arrived from General Graham, with orders for our retreat to the top of the hill, but before we retreated; the colonel made an excellent speech, professing his regard for every man under his command, and at the same time declaring he could keep the town until morning; and if he had not received orders from his superior in command, he would keep possession in spite of the enemy. He added, "We will not retreat without taking every man that is wounded along with us."

We reached the end of the village in, close column, and then called in our detachments, and sent from the column a number of skirmishers, about ten paces in front, who kept up a constant fire on the enemy, who was not more than thirty or forty yards from us. In this position we retreated to the top of the hill: when any man fell, the column halted to ascertain the event, and if only wounded, we carried him along with us. We at last arrived at the top of the hill in good order, and there made a stand: the enemy returned into the town, and made a number of fires, and only left a line of sentries to look out for us.

Having taken our stand on the hill, and finding the enemy did not follow, the rolls were called over, and it was found that in this action, although only about three hundred and sixty strong, we had two captains (one of whom received twenty bayonet wounds) and two lieutenants wounded, one sergeant killed, and forty-five privates killed and wounded, and Lieut. M'Donald taken prisoner. Indeed, we ran considerable hazard of all being taken, for if the French had known our strength, or rather our weakness, they would have used more exertion: by charging three times through the village, we were much more exposed.

General Graham expected no other than that the regiment would have been taken, and he expressed his approbation of our soldier-like conduct. It was not intended that we should have gone into the village to be thus exposed, but to have been posted on the top of the hill which we occupied at this time: the orders were given by mistake. This was my first engagement in Spain.

We had not been long on the hill, when our wine arrived and was served out; but after our fatigues and hard fighting we turned so chilly, that the wine appeared as cold as ice water. After receiving it, the regiment lay down, except a strong advanced guard and piquet, and I got a good sleep until daylight on the bare ground. We then fell in, and kept in readiness for the advance of the enemy; but they did not show any inclination whatever to attack us in this position; if they had, they most probably would have been well beaten: this they anticipated, or they would not have laid all the day within five hundred yards of us without a single shot being exchanged on either side. We had a full view of the enemy's camp; indeed, some of our sentinels were within a very short distance of it.

In the evening of the 21st our regiment was relieved by a brigade of Portuguese infantry, and retreated about a mile to the rear, where we cooked our provisions, and had a good night's rest, although we had neither tents, nor straw, and but few of us had blankets. We laid in the ploughed fields, or anywhere else that our commanders thought proper to place us.

In the evening of the 22nd we began to wash our muskets and clean our accoutrements: about ten o'clock the wood and watering parties had gone out, the foraging parties were forming, and several men had straggled to some distance: when suddenly, the alarm sounded, the regiment formed immediately, and ran in double quick time to our old position, which the enemy was trying to take from us. We had proceeded but a short distance, when we heard the thunder of our cannon playing on the advancing enemy, and in a few minutes, both shot and shells were sent over our regimental column.

Before we reached our station, one of my poor comrades was killed with a musket-shot; being in full run when it happened, he fell with his face to the ground, and expired without a groan. When we got to the summit of the hill, the 68th and the Chasseurs Britanniques formed into a solid square; but the *Chasseurs* being a regiment formed out of every nation in Europe, and many of them deserters from the French Army, we were afraid, if closely attacked, would have broken the column. About twenty yards to our rights the 51st Regiment was drawn up in line, and being on their knees, kept up a steady and well-directed fire on the enemy as they advanced.

On the right of the 51st Light Infantry were six pieces of cannon, which were thundering and pouring death upon the enemy. The 7th Division having possession of the hill, were determined to resist every effort of the enemy, and after several formidable attacks, they gave up all hopes of driving us from the heights, on which we remained until the afternoon, and then retired about six hundred yards to cook our provisions. The loss sustained by our regiment in this skirmish was two men killed and six wounded: it would have been much greater, but we were sheltered by the brow of the hill. The 51st Regiment suffered considerably, having several killed and wounded: Major Rice's horse was shot from under him. Some men belonging to the Chasseurs Britanniques skinned the horse, and sold the flesh to their own men and to the Portuguese at three *vints*, or fourpence halfpenny per lb.

On the morning of the 23rd, although only one night had passed, not a single Frenchman was to be seen in all the plain, having retreated in the direction of the Douro. We then marched back to our camp-ground near Salamanca, where we remained for some time. It was reported that the enemy was in motion to the south of our camp: the 7th Division was marched against them, and our regiment was sent in the front, in extended order, ready to commence the attack, but discovered no enemy; so that in the evening we returned to our old ground.

Now all this time the 6th Division was rapidly advancing in the siege and bombardment of the forts. One evening I went close to the town, out of curiosity, but was not allowed to enter, the sentinel having positive orders to that effect I therefore returned to the camp without gratifying my curiosity.

On the 27th preparations were made in order to storm the forts, whilst one of them was on fire; but before it was attacked, a flag of truce came out, and the governor offered to surrender in a certain number of hours; but General Clinton sent an answer to the effect that it must be surrendered without further delay. The governor not complying, our brave 6th Division commenced the storm, and in a very little time this fort surrendered. After which, the other two gave in, and marched out with the honours of war, the men keeping their knapsacks, and the officers their personal property. The 6th Division suffered greatly, but not so much as might have been expected: Major-General Bowes was killed during the siege.

There was found in these forts a great quantity of clothing, and military stores of every description. The garrison consisted of eight hundred men, and thirty pieces of cannon. The 6th Division being liberated; the whole of the army under Lord Wellington advanced towards the Douro, the main body of the enemy having crossed at Tordesillas, leaving their rearguard at a small town called Rueda, about three miles from the main body. We marched towards the enemy in good order, and in high spirits: one day we went twenty miles over a country that produced nothing but vines: the appearance was exceedingly delightful, for as far as the eye could see, all was a beautiful green: the grapes were not ripe, but we had plenty of what we called green forage, such as peas, lintels, and wheat; so that we suffered but little in this part of the year for the want of provisions.

We arrived at Medina del Campo after a march of three days: it is a very neat town near the Douro, and here we lay in camp until the 14th of July. Whilst in this place, we nearly stripped a convent of its wood to cook with. I have often wondered how or where the Spaniards ever obtained the wood that is used in these convents and churches, for there was none fit for such purposes grown, except at a great distance. I have known on some occasions a large house stripped of every bit of wood, even the floors torn up, and the roofs taken down, for fuel.

While in this camp, we procured our water to cook with from a curious cistern: a large wheel being placed in the well, a number of pots were fixed at a certain distance from each other; the wheel being put in motion, the water emptied itself into a spout, and was then conveyed to every part of the garden: the contrivance was simple and curious. I was several times in the town, but can say little about it, except that it has a market well supplied with bread; vegetables, and fruit.

The division was encamped on the north side of the town, having an advanced guard at the head of each brigade at a considerable distance from the column. One night I was on this guard, and went with several others to obtain lintels or small peas. We arrived at a field where they were ready for leading, and immediately spreading our great coats, commenced thrashing. It was completely dark, but we succeeded in getting our haversacks full, and then returned to our guard. We used to boil them with our meat; and they made a good substitute for bread.

One Sunday evening, several Spanish ladies came into our camp, mounted upon asses. The ladies of Spain frequently ride upon these animals; having no bridles, when they want them to turn, they put out their hand, and push the neck of the beast the way they wish to go: they are very obedient, and seldom refuse going the way they are directed. The Spanish ladies sit on the opposite side to our English females, and often have a man to follow with a long pole as a guard.

On the 15th July the regiment broke up from before Medina del Campo, and marched to La Nava del Rey, and were quartered in the houses during the day; but at sunset we repaired to the fields, and encamped for the night, and in the morning returned to the town: and so on for two or three days and nights. The enemy being near, the division used this precaution for fear of being taken by surprise; but on the last evening we had only just encamped and laid down, when the division was ordered to fall in and march towards Salamanca. This movement was in consequence of the enemy making a vigorous effort to get between us and the city of Rodrigo. We continued our march until daylight, and then heard the roar of their cannon.

After making a short halt. We marched to the top of a rising ground, but were immediately countermarched, and continued to retreat. The enemy's guns were playing during the greater part of the day, and several skirmishes took place between both infantry and cavalry: I saw them at different times as we marched along. At length we took up a position directly opposite the hill on which the enemy was posted, and sent out our wood and watering parties, received our provisions and began to cook them.

During this day's march several men expired in the ranks from excessive heat and fatigue. This was a day of suffering, nearly twenty-four hours marching, and having scarcely a moment to breathe. We remained in this camp until the evening of the 19th, and then moved to the right of our lines: during this manoeuvre we came to a run of deep water, and having no bridge, were obliged to jump over, the stream being wide, and the men weak, several, of them jumped in; but I managed over very well. We continued our march about three miles further, and encamped in a wood, but had only just lighted our fires, when we were ordered forwards, being enjoined to keep the strictest silence.

Nothing could exceed the deathlike stillness; no man daring to speak. We at length arrived at the camp of the 1st Division, which was within one mile of the enemy's camp. The brigade immediately piled arms and laid down until daylight, when the divisions formed and waited the attack of Marshal Marmont. I certainly expected that in a few minutes we should have been sharply engaged, but instead of this, the enemy broke up their camp, formed column, and marched to a ridge of hills, their drums and bands playing as though they were going to a general field-day. I saw the head of their column ascend the hill and march in the direction of Ciudad Rodrigo. We marched in two lines parallel with them, having only to halt and front, and we were ready to receive them.

We were not more than a mile from each other, sometimes not so much: every now and then the enemy unlimbered their guns, and fired on the British lines; but no execution was done, with the exception of one poor woman, who was killed by a cannon-shot. It was an extraordinary and grand sight to see two armies drawn up ready for battle, and manoeuvring during a whole day, without fighting. In the evening we reached the termination of the hill; the enemy then moved off and encamped, but we continued our march in the direction of Salamanca until dusk, when we encamped in an open country. I was immediately sent on the advanced guards which had received strict orders to keep a good look out, for the enemy could not be more than four miles distant. I went on sentry, and had frequently to put my ear to the ground to listen for them, a practice very common with the advanced guard of an army.

On the 21st we got within sight of Salamanca, and halted on the banks of the River Tormes, where we cooked our dinners, but had the greatest difficulty in obtaining fuel, having to gather dried cow-dung, thistles, or an thing that would burn. When dinner was over, we fell in, and, fording the river, marched into a wood five miles from the above-mentioned place, and encamped about eight o'clock at night. We had not, however, been long at rest, before a most alarming storm came on: the thunder in awful claps echoed through the wood; the flashes of lightning were vivid, and quick in succession; the rain fell in torrents, and, what added to our distress, was, we were exposed to the open air, not having a tent or anything else to cover us.

Several of the cavalry horses broke from their stakes, and caused great confusion in the different regiments of cavalry. The suspense we had been in during the last few days, being in expectation of an engagement every hour, made our situation extremely uncomfortable; indeed, at this period the enemy was within two miles of our advanced guard. Notwithstanding the great rains which had fallen during the nighty I contrived to keep myself dry, by getting directly under the arm of a large tree, and creeping under the blanket of an old comrade, who is now fixed in business in this county. It was astonishing to see the cheerfulness of the men: I have known them tell tales, sing songs, and crack their jokes, in the midst of danger, and when it was uncertain whether they would live to see another day over. About midnight the storm ceased, the morning was beautiful, the sun rose without a cloud, and everything had a most enchanting appearance.

CHAPTER 10

Battle of Salamanca

Early on the morning of the 22nd July, we heard the firing of the advanced guard, and in less than ten minutes our regiment, being light infantry, was, ordered forward; having reached the front, we saw the French piquets advancing on ours, and both were sharply engaged. In a moment the left wing was ordered to the front: no sooner did our advanced piquets perceive that they were supported by such a number of light troops, than they advanced on the French piquets, and drove them in confusion to the summit of a high hill, but the enemy receiving strong reinforcements, bore down on my brave comrades, who contested every inch with them. At this period a general came to the front, to see how things were going on: in a fit of passion he enquired, "Who commands here?"

The answer was, "General Hope."

He said, "Where is he? the whole of the advanced piquets will be taken prisoners."

General Hope came up at the time, but did not appear at all afraid that the men would be taken: he sent one of his *aides-de-camp* with directions for a squadron of light dragoons to support the skirmishers immediately: they came forward, and had only just taken their stand when one of them, a youth of about twenty-one years of age, was killed. The enemy now retired to the top of the hill, and brought six pieces of cannon to play on us. About this time the watering parties of the 7th Division came to the valley for a supply of water: the French guns began to play on these unarmed and defenceless men; but not one of them was hurt, although shot and shell fell thickly amongst them. After this the enemy continued firing on us for some hours. In this skirmish Major Miller and several privates were wounded, and one of the latter had to undergo amputation.

We remained in this position until afternoon, but were not allowed to take off our accoutrements. About three o'clock the 95th Rifle Corps arriving, took our places, and we immediately marched off to join the division. About this time the cannonading commenced: the French had nearly one hundred pieces of cannon firing on our army, which was forming for the attack: we had about sixty pieces; and the thunder of these one hundred and sixty guns was terrible, and beggars description.

Having joined the division, and taken our place on the left of the first brigade; we halted a few minutes, and then advanced to the spot where our artillery were stationed. We now came into an open plain, and were completely exposed to the fire of the enemy's artillery. Along this plain a division of the army was stationed: I think it was the 4th Division: the men laid down in order to escape the shot and shells, the army not yet being ready to advance. As our regiment was marching along the rear of this division, I saw a shell fall on one of the men, which killed him on the spot; a part of the shell tore his knapsack to pieces, and I saw it flying in the air after the shell had burst.

The shot of the foe now began to take effect on us. As we were marching in open column to take our position, one of the supernumerary sergeants, whose name was Dunn, had both his legs shot from under him, and died in a few minutes. Shortly after, a shot came and took away the leg and thigh, with part of the body, of a young officer named Finukin: to have seen him, and heard the screams of his servant, would have almost rended a heart of stone: he was a good master, an excellent officer, and was lamented by all who knew him. The next thing I have to relate is of the company which was directly in our front, commanded by Captain Gough; a cannon-ball came, and striking the right of the company, made the arms gingle and fly in pieces like broken glass.

One of the bayonets was broken off, and sent through a man's neck with as much force as though it had been done by a strong and powerful hand. I saw the man pull it out, and singular to relate, he recovered: three others were also wounded. About this time, I had a narrow escape from a cannon-ball, which passed within a few inches of me: although it was nearly spent, yet, had it struck me, I should have been either killed or wounded by it.

After this, we formed column of quarter distance and several shells fell into our column, and did execution: one shell I shall ever remember: we were in the act of lying down, that it might burst, and do no mischief: the colonel cried out, "It is a shot!" and we stood up im-

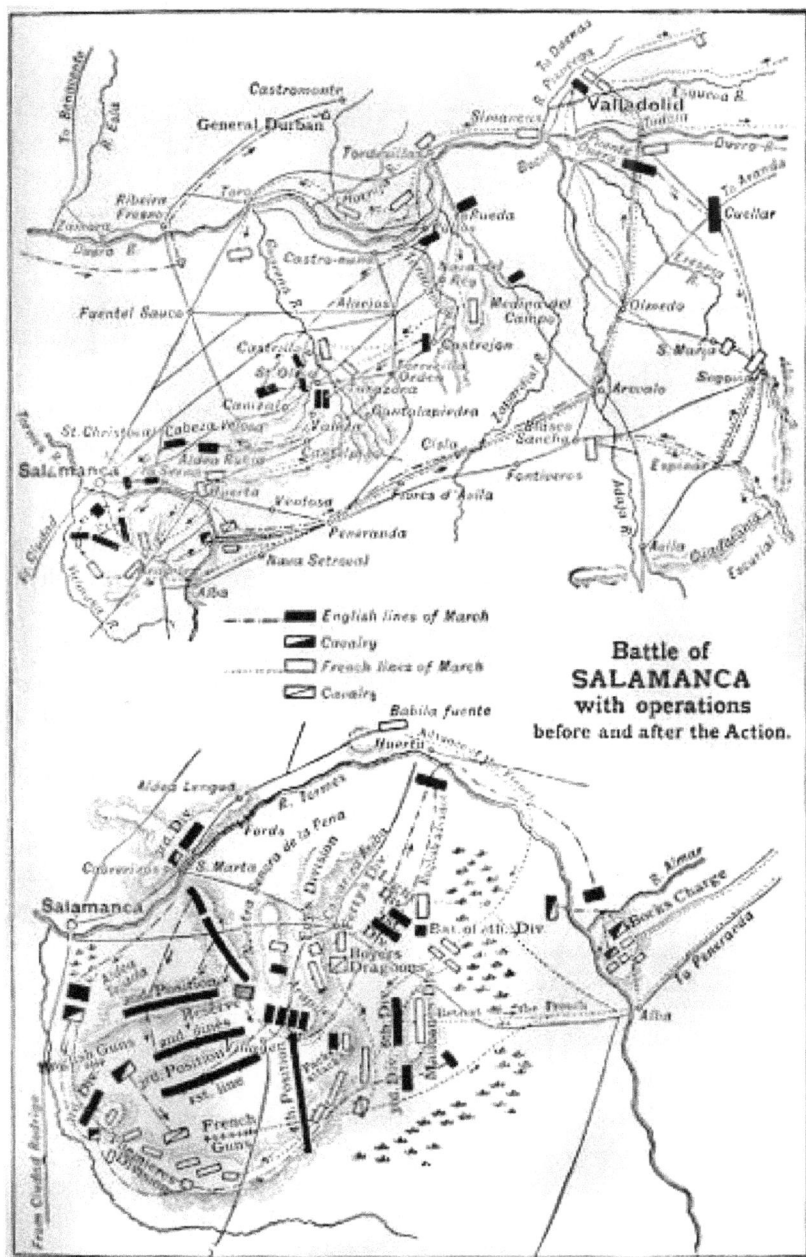

Battle of
SALAMANCA
with operations
before and after the Action.

English lines of March
Cavalry
French lines of March
Cavalry

mediately; but, while in the act of rising, the shell burst in the midst of the regimental column, and, astonishing to relate, not a man received an injury by it! We now took our position, and waited the signal to advance.

About half-past four o'clock Lord Wellington came into the front of our division, and pulled off his hat, our army gave three cheers, and advanced on the French, who were ready to receive us: we continued to advance some time without firing a shot; at length the firing of both armies commenced in such a way as I had never heard before; it was like the long roll of a hundred drums without an interval.

Both armies fought with courage and determination; and it was doubtful for some time which would gain the day: at last, the enemy gave way in all directions, and we completely beat them out of the field with dreadful carnage. Their loss in this memorable battle was eleven pieces of cannon, several ammunition waggons, two eagles, and six colours. The French commander in chief lost his arm; it was astonishing how soon we heard of his being wounded. We took one general officer, three colonels, three lieutenant-colonels, one hundred and thirty officers, and about seven thousand privates. Their loss in killed and wounded must have been very great indeed.

The total loss of the Allied Armies in this desperate action was six hundred and ninety-four men killed, four thousand two hundred and seventy wounded, and two hundred and thirty-six missing; making a grand total of five thousand two hundred, beside what were lost in pursuit of the enemy; and to which may be added the loss of the 6th Division at the forts in the city, Major-General le Marchant was killed; Lieutenant-Generals Cole, Leith, Cotton, and Major-General Alten, were wounded. I think it was the 61st Regiment that had only three officers left, and the command devolved upon the adjutant, who had been the sergeant-major. The loss sustained by our regiment was one subaltern and one sergeant killed, one major, two captains, and forty privates killed and wounded, making our total loss near this place ninety-three out of our small regiment, which was not more than three hundred strong in the field.

After the battle, we encamped on that part of the field where the carnage had been the most dreadful, and actually piled our arms amongst the dead and dying. We immediately sent six men from each company to collect the wounded, and carry them to a small village, where doctors were in attendance to dress their wounds. It really was distressing to hear the cries and moans of the wounded and dying, whose sufferings were augmented by the Portuguese plunderers stripping several of them naked. We took a poor Frenchman, who had been stripped by an unfeeling Portuguese: the adjutant gave him a shirt, an old jacket and trowsers, and sent him to the village hospital.

In a short time, the baggage and women arrived, and amongst them the wife of Sergeant Dunn, who was killed at the commencement of the action: the poor woman was nearly frantic when she heard her husband was no more. Her loss certainly was great; but in less than a week she took up with a sergeant of the same company, whose name was Gilbert Hinds, with whom she has lived ever since. This poor woman was unlucky, for she had lost five husbands: Hinds is her sixth!

On the morning of the 23rd we marched in pursuit of the enemy, crossed the River Tormes, and encamped on the very spot where the enemy had been resting. On the 24th we moved off again, and came to a place where there had been a desperate action between the enemy's rear and our advanced guard; the particulars are as follow: The heavy German brigade of cavalry having taken a column of the enemy who had laid down their arms, immediately rode after another column of the enemy, without leaving a sufficient guard with their prisoners, who immediately took their arms again, and commenced a desperate firing on the conquerors, many of whom were killed and wounded. The Germans turned on them with fury, and put a vast number to the sword. There were about two thousand stand of arms laid by the roadside, beside the caps, cocked hats, &c. of the men who had been killed, The conquerors had buried their dead, but we saw several dead Frenchmen lying by the side of the road as we marched along, no one offering to bury them.

We continued our pursuit after the enemy, leaving Medina del Campo on our left, crossed several rivers, and on the 27th reached Olmedo, and encamped in a wood of firs near a large river, on the banks of which were plums in abundance. On the 28th we halted in this beautiful place. Next day we marched a long and tedious journey through several good-looking towns, but I cannot give their names; and about three o'clock in the afternoon the division halted at the entrance of a very extensive wood. On the 30th we proceeded left in front, and encamped in the same wood. August the 2nd, we arrived at the other side, and halted on the 3rd, 4th, and 5th; and on the 6th marched towards a ridge of mountains, which seemed to darken the whole side of the country. These mountains run past the Escurial, a

Battle of Salamanca

very great palace of the Spanish king: the tops of some of these mountains are white; I should suppose they are covered with snow.

On the 7th we encamped within one mile of the city of Segovia, but were not allowed to enter without a pass. This place is large, well-built, and stands on a rising ground; it is walled round, and has several churches and public buildings. There is also a noble aqueduct, consisting of great number of arches, the water being conducted from the mountains above mentioned. There are several manufactures carried on here with considerable success.

8th. We again joined in pursuit of the enemy, who was at no great distance from us. This day we passed one of the king's hunting palaces, and encamped in one of the most enchanting places I ever saw. We had only just piled our arms, when a fine deer started; several of our men ran after him, but the more they ran and shouted the swifter he fled, and was soon out of sight. The camp-ground was as smooth as though it had been rolled with a heavy roller: here and there a cluster of young oaks beautified the scene, and made it most delightful; and to us they were excellent summer-houses: it was indeed the most comfortable camp we had during the whole of the campaign.

9th. We marched up hill nearly all the day, and climbed over a great part of these vast mountains, which had been in view so many days, and encamped in a small valley on the top of them. Here we received a quantity of chocolate, salt, and soap, which were very acceptable indeed. This evening the fire from the cooking-places communicated with the bents, or dried grass, and spread through the camp with astonishing rapidity; but the men ran, and, cutting boughs from the trees, in a few minutes succeeded in beating it out, so that no damage was done either to us or to the woods.

Early the next morning we were again in motion, and continued our movements until we reached the extremity of these mountains, where we had a distinct view of Madrid, the capital of Spain: and as we marched uphill the day before, we now began to descend; and reaching a plain, encamped where water was plentiful. This day a severe contest took place with our advanced guard, consisting of the German brigade of cavalry, a regiment of Portuguese, and a brigade of horse artillery.

The enemy's rear guard attacked the Portuguese piquet, which giving way, left our guns exposed: the enemy advanced in great numbers, and pressed so hard upon our German horse, that they had only a few minutes to mount and form, before the enemy was upon them; but the Germans fought well, stood their ground, and succeeded in beating the enemy back; but the captain of the artillery, several of his men, and three guns, were taken: in a few days, however, we retook them. The loss in killed and wounded was great on both sides.

On the 11th we commenced our movements, and encamped within thirteen miles of the capital, and close to the village where the advanced posts had been engaged. The 12th, we moved off early, and suffered much from the paved roads. This day Lord Wellington passed our division on his way to the capital: when we were within five miles of Madrid, the people came out in great numbers to meet us: the day being very hot, some of our men fainted, but the Spaniards immediately took them under their care, giving them wine or spirits; a great number of melons were also distributed to the men in the ranks. The people shouted and rejoiced as we marched along, and the bands of the different regiments enlivened the scene by frequently playing the "Downfall of Paris;" the colours were displayed, and we frequently gave three cheers: indeed, there was little else but shouts and bursts of approbation for the last two miles.

We at length arrived at the gates, the streets were crowded with the populace, and the windows occupied by ladies; the tops of the houses near the gate were also crowded. We marched along the streets amidst the rending and exulting shouts of "*Viva los Ingleses!*" or "Long live the English!" The bells of the different churches rang, the ladies waved their handkerchiefs from the windows, and every countenance beamed with joy, welcoming their deliverers: in some instances, the Spaniards embraced the soldiers. We halted in front of the new palace: here we shouted and cheered the people in return. Ours was the first Regiment of British infantry that entered Madrid: after waiting a few minutes, the whole of our division marched into a convent, which was the largest I ever saw, affording room and convenience for nine regiments; and in the centre of the square stood a fountain which nearly supplied the whole with good water.

In the afternoon of the 13th the first brigade was ordered to the field, to punish a man, who, in conjunction with two others, had been long under sentence and confinement, for sacrilege in a village in Portugal. Two of the prisoners were present on this occasion, the other was sick in one of the hospitals. When the decision of the court martial was read, one of the two was liberated; but the other was ordered to strip: he was tied up, and received eight hundred lashes by the strongest drummers and buglers in the brigade. The poor fellow stood it very well, and on his way home to the convent the people would have loaded him with money, but our commander would not suffer him to take it: it was astonishing how soon the man recovered after such a severe flogging.

We returned to the convent, but instead of going in, were marched off to attack the Retiro, a very strong fort garrisoned by two thousand five hundred of the enemy. This night Madrid was illuminated, the bells rang, and nothing but joy and rejoicing were going forward among the Spaniards. We assembled in front of one of the public buildings, and were told off into detachments, for the attack of the fort. I and five others were sent to join a party of Germans under the command of a German officer, our colonel giving us strict orders to do our duty, and to behave like soldiers. We moved off about ten o'clock at night, after receiving orders. to keep the strictest silence. Passing through several streets, lanes, and squares, we at length got clear of the city, but in crossing the fields, one of the men fell headlong into a hole, and two or three others fell over him: by this accident the enemy heard us. We got within a few yards of the gate, and received a volley from them, which wounded four out of the thirty men of our detachment.

Such was the consternation which this volley caused, that the whole of the Germans, with two of our men, gave way; the officer, a very courageous man, ran after them, calling them back. I and two others stood our ground, and began to fire upon the enemy, who returned the compliment. The officer coming back with his Germans, took a musket from one of the men, and fired several shots into the place: at this time the main body of our regiment attacked the large gate, drove it in, and established themselves within the outer walls; when an officer was dispatched with orders from our colonel, that we were to break in also, and take possession of the inner gate.

It was now midnight, and so dark that we could scarcely see our way. We formed, however, and marched up to the gate, but found the enemy had fled into the fort, leaving the sentry-box laid across the gateway, to prevent our entering, but we instantly broke down the piles, and took possession of the outwork, we then sent a small piquet to examine the interior, and found they had fled in such haste, that they had left a part of their clothings cooking utensils, &c.

In the morning our colonel sent orders for our detachment to take possession of a redoubt: we marched for that purpose, but were forced back by the cannon of the enemy. I had two or three very narrow escapes, for a piece of a shell fell within twelve inches of my head. The fire of the enemy was terrible for some time. About this period. Lord Wellington came to our gate, and took a view of the fort, and then ordered us to show ourselves: the moment the French saw us, they opened a very heavy fire of musketry; in consequence of which, His Lordship ordered us to retreat to the gate, and about ten o'clock everything was ready for a general storm. A flag of truce was sent, with proposals to the British commander, which were accepted, and the French marched out of the garrison with the honours of war.

The whole of the garrison consisted of two thousand five hundred and six officers and privates, who particularly requested that the English might march them prisoners to Lisbon, in preference to either the Spaniards or the Portuguese: indeed, such was the spirit of the Spaniards at this period, that it would have been dangerous to have sent them with the prisoners. We found in this fort two hundred pieces of cannon, nine hundred barrels of gun pounder, twenty thousand muskets, and about fifty thousand suits of clothing, beside a very great quantity of provisions, ammunition, wine, spirits, and military stores of every description.

I obtained as many things in the fort as amounted to two pounds or more. Our colonel was made governor of this garrison, and very kindly sent every man a pair of French shoes. We returned to the convent after capturing this rich and valuable fort; and the two men who ran away had liked to have had their heads shaved for their cowardice; but one of them being a sort of idiot, both were pardoned, after receiving a severe reprimand.

We halted in Madrid until the 21st of August, which was a very great treat, as we had commonly to lay out of doors without tents. Whilst here, I saw Titus Burgess, William Kirk, and several other young men of the 3rd or King's Own Dragoons, natives also of Louth.

I cannot leave Madrid without giving a short description of it. It has eighteen parishes, thirty-five convents for monks, and thirty-one for nuns; thirty-nine colleges, hospitals, or houses of charity; seven or eight thousand dwelling houses, and nearly two hundred thousand inhabitants. There is also a very fine market-place, where the bull-fights used to take place: this market is well supplied with bread, meat, vegetables, and fruits of various sorts. In short, Madrid is a very handsome city, being built chiefly of stone: its length is about three miles, and its breadth about two. The inhabitants dress much like the English; and some of the shops are very good. There is a description of cook shops here, which sell fried pepper that has the taste of meat: it is the pod that is fried while in a green state. Bread is also good, cheap, and plentiful.

The people in Spain and Portugal do not eat so much flesh meat as the people in England, but live more on vegetables, fruit, or oil; so that good meat is scarce and dear. I have often seen from twenty to thirty acres of onions in one plat, and from thirty to forty acres of cabbages, I remember, when at Salamanca, that the Spanish soldiers were constantly boiling cabbages: they used to put onions, oil, pepper, and salt among them, and thus eat altogether.

The houses in Madrid are generally good, but in most of the places where I have been they have no glass windows: they have shutters instead, so that at night, or in bad weather, they close them. The winter in these parts is short, indeed in the south of Spain it is like our spring.

CHAPTER 11

The Enemy Advances

On the 21st of August, we left the Spanish capital, and marched for Escurial, where we arrived after a march of two days, and took up our quarters in an uninhabited inn, and remained until the 1st of September. In this place there is a palace belonging to the Spanish monarch, which is supposed to be one of the grandest buildings in Spain. Part of the army was quartered in the out-offices and stables of this magnificent edifice.

Escurial is situated on the side of a vast mountain, and may be seen from Madrid, distant seven leagues. There were about twenty-five thousand of the allies quartered in this town; but there was abundance of room, so that all were well accommodated, receiving a daily supply of French provisions from Madrid. While in Escurial, the captain who commanded the regiment was severe in the extreme. I have often trembled when I have had to be inspected by him, although I always passed his severe scrutiny. He did not command long, for Colonel Johnson came from Madrid, and took the command from him. Although the colonel was an Irishman, yet he was as good an officer as ever commanded a regiment: he was very hot in his temper, but was soon appeased: he was an officer that loved his men, and could not be happy unless they were comfortable, indeed, he has often been known to shed tears when we were short of provisions, and could not obtain them for money.

September the 1st, we left Escurial at four in the morning, and encamped in a small wood. On the 2nd we marched over this vast chain of mountains, which can be distinctly seen more than sixty miles, and took up our quarters in a small town. On the 3rd we arrived at Arevalo, a smart little town, with an excellent market; 4th, encamped in the neighbourhood of Olmedo; and on the 7th reached Valladolid, where we got sight of the enemy. Here we halted three days, being encamped close to a branch of the Douro. At this time grapes were ripe, but they were on the opposite side of the river, this, however, did not prevent us from obtaining a supply, for some of the men, taking off their clothes, swam over, ran a mile or two, filled their haversacks, and returned with their valuable cargo. Grapes and bread make an excellent repast, and are both good and wholesome, affording considerable nourishment.

In this part of Spain, and all along the banks of the Douro, there are abundance of grapes, apples, oranges, lemons, sweet almonds, pears, and plums; indeed, nothing could exceed the fruitfulness of these banks, for at least sixty miles, so that all the country within the district of Valladolid, and on the south of the Douro, has a most delightful appearance.

Valladolid is a large, compact, and handsome place. Columbus; the discoverer of America, died here. It is twenty leagues from Burgos, twenty from Salamanca, and perhaps about thirty from Madrid. On the 10th we again marched in pursuit of the enemy, who was at no great distance from us, and encamped within twelve miles of Valladolid. On the 11th we marched through a small market-town, the inhabitants of which lined the streets and windows, and shouted "*Viva los Ingleses!*" until some of them were quite exhausted. One poor woman came out of her house in a great hurry, and began to shout "*Viva los Franceses!*" or "Long live the French!" From this it appears, that the Spaniards, used to cheer the French Army, as well as ours; but the woman had forgotten which army it was, and perhaps to her it was of little importance.

We encamped about two miles from this place, and on the 12th our headquarters were near Torquemada. We continued to follow the French Army, who retreated slowly before us: I think we seldom marched more than eight miles a day. On the 14th we encamped in a grape-field, which extended over more than two hundred acres of ground; so that we were well supplied with excellent grapes. The valleys produce wheat, barley, beans, and other grain. We had also good pastures for our horses and mules, and a plentiful supply of water, but wood was very scarce, there being little to be found; except poplar, which will not burn without a great deal of trouble.

On the 16th we had some hard marching and manoeuvring, the enemy having taken a strong position on each side of the road leading to Burgos. Our division moved to the front, for the purpose of dislodging them from the heights on the left, whilst another division was sent to the opposite heights for the same purpose: the cavalry, a strong body of infantry, and artillery, moved along the valley, and after a little skirmishing; the enemy marched off in the direction of Burgos, leaving us in possession of the hills. It was a beautiful day, and to see the two armies marching along, each having a line of skirmishers in its front, was grand; but to observe our cavalry scouting their rear, and how the enemy scampered off, was very diverting, especially as few lives were lost on the occasion.

In the evening we halted near a small village within sight of Burgos, and the next day encamped within two miles of the castle. The main body of the enemy marched in the direction of Vittoria, leaving a strong garrison in the castle, to which had been added a formidable out-work on the hill of St. Michael. Here we lay for two or three days, and had a grand view of an attack made upon the redoubt by the first division: in the second attempt it was taken, with the loss of four hundred men on our part; but out of five hundred of the enemy, only sixty-three were taken, the others escaped into the castle.

The particulars are as follow: seventy-one killed, three hundred and twenty-three wounded, and sixteen missing, with four captains and six lieutenants wounded. The assistant quartermaster general, and two officers of the 42nd Regiment, were killed; so that our loss in this small affair was very great. The Portuguese are included in this calculation.

On the 21st we marched round and encamped on the other side of the city, between the besiegers and the enemy, where we lay until the 26th, when we moved off to a village called Villa Tormes, about twenty miles above Burgos, on the Vittoria road. This day, the whole of the division encamped together, but afterwards separated into brigades;—our brigade encamped on the side of a hill south of the main road, and under a few scattered oak trees, where we made *wigwams* or huts of the boughs; but from the want of proper materials, could not make them water-proof. There were not more than three huts that would turn the rain, so that for twenty-four days or more we were exposed to the constant dribbling rains, which had now set in. Some days, indeed, it rained all day without intermission.

What made our situation most uncomfortable and unpleasant, was, we were almost naked, for we were nearly out of all the necessaries so essential to our comfort; such as stockings, shoes, shirts, blankets, watchcoats, and trousers; and, what was worse than all, it now began to be very cold, for when the rain ceased, there was a frost almost every night, so that we were nearly perished. While in this place I heard distinctly the report of one of the great guns from Burgos castle, although the distance was twenty miles. I understood it was a sixty-eight pounder, one of the largest that is used; indeed, there are very few larger than forty-four pounders used in garrisons. The besiegers made but slow progress in the reduction of the castle: if our first division had had a few of these sixty-eight pounders, they would, have soon broken down the walls, and reduced this strong and formidable fortification.

October 14th. Our regiment and the 51st left the camp above mentioned, and advanced to two small villages, called Upper and Lower Monasterio, on the left of the Vittoria road. The situation of Upper Monasterio is very romantic; the village stands between two high hills, and a little river runs through the valley. Here is produced good flax, which the people manufacture into cloth: the population does not exceed two hundred. Here we had very strong guards to mount, and a regular working party, who were employed in building a breastwork across the valley, in order to check the advance of the enemy, who we expected would make an attempt to raise the siege of Burgos.

We were right in our expectation, for the enemy soon made their, appearance. On their approach, the working parties hid their tools in a pond of deep water, and took to their arms; but the two regiments marched to the heights in the rear of the village above mentioned, and there waited the event; but nothing of consequence took place. We remained on the heights until seven o'clock in the evening, and then returned into Upper Monasterio. We were not allowed to go to our quarters, but the two regiments marched into the church, in order that they might be ready if the enemy should advance suddenly upon the outposts.

To this church there was but one door, and a dim taper was suspended from the roof, which gave so little light, that we could only just see to lay down. The church had no pews, or the two regiments could not have been accommodated with room sufficient. I laid down under one of the side altars: but previous to this period, I had been under confinement for taking a little wheat from a peasant, who complained to an officer of the 51st Regiment, and he ordered me to the guard-house. I remained a prisoner three days, and missed a deal of hard duty and stormy weather, for it rained nearly all the time I was in the guardroom.

But this afternoon the prisoners were ordered to join their respective companies, and I never heard any more about the wheat; indeed, our officers knew we were hungry, or we should not have troubled ourselves with raw wheat, or anything of the kind. I have known some of the officers, who would have gladly helped themselves, if it could have been done with secrecy: hunger often caused us to do things, which we should have been ashamed to do, if we had had plenty: but this was not the case, for we have often been working and watching the enemy eighteen hours out of the twenty-four, having only the same scanty allowance, and sometimes not that.

This evening, as we returned into the village, all the ovens were occupied in baking bread, as we thought for the French Army; for before this, we could obtain bread neither for love nor money. The Spaniards have often supplied the enemy, and left us destitute of that essential article, although we were fighting their battles, and doing all in our power to free them from the yoke of Buonaparte; but at the bottom, the Spaniards in this part did not like us, and indeed our commanders were too easy with them, for they should have insisted on a supply, as the French frequently did, for they would either have bread or money, and this might be one reason why the enemy was supplied with such promptitude.

But to return to the church: it had, as I said before, only one entrance, over which we had a sentry placed, in order that nothing might be taken out. About midnight the sentinel had fallen into a sound sleep, and in the midst of the awful stillness of the night, one of the 51st Regiment exclaimed, with all the confidence of truth, that the enemy was coming in at the door. "Here they are!" said he, in an apparent fright. It is impossible for me to describe the dreadful confusion that ensued: some of the men began to load their muskets, and others to fix their bayonets; saying, "Charge, charge out of the door!" The adjutant being the only officer in the church, commanded us to load, sayings he was determined at all events to brush out at the door.

At length a person ventured out, and in a moment returned, saying, the alarm was false, for there was no individual near the church. When inquiry was made, it was found that the man who had given the alarm had been dreaming that the enemy had surrounded the church, and that we were in imminent danger of being taken prisoners. This explanation allayed our fears, and we again laid down to rest; but at three o'clock in the morning we left the church, and took a position on the hills, about a mile from the town, and waited until day-light, when the enemy made their appearance on the opposite hills. It was a very wet morning, and every man was as wet as though he had been dipped in a river. About ten o'clock we received our biscuit, which had been so soaked with rain, that every man's allowance appeared nearly as big again as it usually was.

We remained on the heights until the afternoon, looking at each other; our sentinels being within two hundred yards of the enemy's, and neither appearing inclined to advance. At four o'clock, however, two brigades of cavalry arriving, took our ground; and we then retired about three miles into Villa Tormes, and were quartered in the church: here we lay on the bare stones, with little or no covering. In the morning we left the church, formed on a green near the town, and piled our arms; but were not allowed to pull off our accoutrements. In about an hour, orders came for our advance; but we had not proceeded more than a mile, when we were ordered to retreat to the same place, where we piled arms, and began to cook our provisions.

We remained here until afternoon, when we were directed to fall in, for the enemy's advanced guard was within a short distance of the village. We accordingly advanced to meet them; but the enemy being so strong and formidable, we retreated through Villa Tormes, and took up a position on the bank of a small river, which our people had made deeper by damming it below the town; but scarcely had we lined ourselves on the bank, before we were attacked by the advanced guard. We immediately commenced a brisk fire on them, which continued until our pieces were so hot, that we could scarcely hold them. This checked the enemy, and kept them back for some time; but their skirmishers being supported by a strong regiment of infantry, now advanced to the edge of the river in great force, and compelled us to retreat towards the top of the hill, on which we had been previously encamped.

While in the act of retreating, we kept up a heavy, constant, and well-directed fire; but notwithstanding this, the enemy crossed the river and followed us nearly to the summit of the hill. Suddenly, however, six pieces of cannon, which had been hidden behind the hill, unknown either to us or to the enemy, were dragged to the summit, where they opened a terrible fire, which caused them to retreat in consternation: we followed, and galled them severely, forcing them to retrace their steps over the river faster than they came: after which, we retired to the top of the hill, and piled arms.

About a mile to our right, our second brigade was sharply engaged: they had two pieces of cannon, and succeeded in beating the enemy back. Our regiment being now stationed on the side of the hill, had a grand sight: the enemy's regiment that supported their skirmishers continued still under the brow of the opposite hill, not being aware that a division of British infantry, four or five regiments of cavalry, and two brigades of artillery, were so near to them: indeed, our cavalry got within three hundred yards before they were perceived. As soon as the enemy's regiment knew their situation, off they scampered through Villa Tormes, but had only just passed through the town, when the cannon of the fifth Division began to play upon them: it now began to be dusk, but we heard our cavalry charging the enemy several times, driving them nearly to Monasterio.

Our loss in this skirmish was two men wounded, one of whom had to undergo amputation. I saw the doctor perform the operation; but the poor man survived only a few days. The other man never left the regiments. During this skirmish, I had a very narrow escape: I was in the act of speaking to my comrade, who had been struck with a spent ball, when a shot passed so near my mouth that I felt the wind it occasioned. The shots fired by the French infantry were numerous, but no man was hurt by them: the two men above mentioned, were wounded by a cannon-shot.

Next morning there was no movement: we remained during the day in the same place, and saw the smoke arise from the enemy's camp, which was about six miles from ours. Here our further advance was checked, for the enemy having been strongly reinforced, seemed determined to fight, or force us to retreat. Owing to these and other circumstances. Lord Wellington thought it prudent to retreat into Portugal: he might, indeed, have fought the enemy on this ground; but he could not have maintained it to advantage, his supplies and hospitals being so distant, and the winter having already made its appearance.

CHAPTER 12

Reaches Valladolid

On the evening of the 20th October, we began the memorable retreat from Burgos, but left a man of each company behind us to keep the fires burnings in order to deceive the enemy, that they might not know we had commenced our retreat. In about an hour, the men left with the fires joined us: we marched all the night, passed Burgos castle towards morning, and continued to retreat until we had marched nearly forty miles, being fatigued to that degree, that several of the men actually dropped down in the ranks.

The next morning, we moved again, marched thirty-two miles, and encamped in a large grape-field, at the edge of which, and within two hundred yards of our camp, were several wine-vaults. I was very tired, laid myself down, and fell into a sound sleep, but was awakened by the constant rattling of canteens, and the cry of "Who wants water?" One of the men gave me a drink, and instead of water, it proved to be wine.

"Where did you get it?" was the enquiry.

"Over there," said the man, pointing to the place. I immediately got up, and set off to seek the wine-vaults, and soon found one; but the Spaniard who owned it was watching: he however directed me to another. When I got there, I found several soldiers, one of whom had a lighted stick, with which we descended into the cellar, and obtained as much wine as we wanted. In the morning, so many of the men were drunk, that it astonished the colonel and officers, who could not imagine how or where the men had obtained the liquor. I kept myself sober; indeed, I was very ill, for the two last days' marches had nearly overcome my strength.

The wine-vaults in this part of Spain are curiously constructed, being cut out of the solid ground. The materials for the casks are prepared, and then put together inside the vaults. Some of them are very large, and will hold three thousand gallons and upwards. The doorways of the vaults are so narrow, that one man only can enter at once, and he must go sideways. Some of our men, while in these vaults, pulled out the plug or bung of one of the casks; the wine rushing out, caused such a strong fume, that they could not get the bung in again: the whole of the wine ran out; and the next morning one man was found drowned, and floating in the wine! What must have been the feelings of the poor inhabitants, when they visited their cellars, and found them emptied of their valuable contents!

This morning we moved off in the direction of Palencia, the enemy being close upon our rear. At Torquemado our rear-uard had a most desperate action with the enemy, who pressed so hard upon them that we were in danger of losing a brigade of light dragoons; but Colonel Halket, with his brigade of German infantry, succeeded in beating the enemy back with very great loss. The Colonel of the 16th Light Dragoons, however, was taken prisoner on this occasion.

October 23rd. Our division pushed on to Valladolid, in order to intercept the enemy at that place. We suffered dreadfully on this retreat. The first day we marched nearly forty miles, on the second, thirty-two miles; and on the third, nearly thirty miles. Men frequently fell down in the ranks quite exhausted, and in some instances, I have known them expire on the spot. I have often seen three or four fine-looking horses fall down and die in the course of a day. This evening we reached the neighbourhood of Valladolid, and encamped; on the 24th we crossed the bridge, formed on the other side of the river, and threw up a breast-work opposite the bridge.

The miners also began to bore, in order to blow it up: they bored down to the foundations of the middle arches, and filled the place with powder, having a quantity ready to lay a train; so that whenever the enemy attempted to cross the bridge, we could send it into the air. Here we remained three days. This day I went on guard about eight hundred yards above the bridge, in a beautiful garden, the end of which was washed by this river. Sentries were placed on its banks to watch the enemy, who might have got over, there being a large boat on the other side; but our business was to fire on the man who attempted to remove it.

On the 26th the enemy appeared on the other side of the river in great force, and placed twelve pieces of cannon on a hill opposite the bridge, from which they played on us; but having some strong buildings and breastworks in our front, there was little or no execution done. While in these gardens, I went to some distance to obtain potatoes; but the garden to which I went was completely exposed to the enemy, who, when they saw two or three of us together, fired on us with musketry. We were not to be intimidated by their fire, neither would we move a jot until we had obtained a supply; and, strange as it may appear, not one man received a wound, although sixty or a hundred had visited this garden on the same errand. The only person killed at this place was a woman of the 51st Regiment, who had heedlessly approached too near the bridge.

In the afternoon of the 27th, after a severe cannonading on both sides, orders were given to blow up the bridge, and retreat to Tordesillas. The bridge immediately blew up into the air, and we began our retreat; and the enemy's cavalry entered one end of the market place, as we went out of the other. We marched until dark, and encamped near the Douro, It was a grand sight to see the contending armies on the sides of the river, frequently within one mile of each other; indeed, both armies came to the Douro for water, and frequently at the same time. We had taken the precaution, however, to send a number of men to blow up the bridge at Tordesillas, if occasion should require such a measure. The next day we marched through a delightful country: on our right was the Douro, and the enemy marching on its north bank frequently within sight. The river in this part is wide and deep, so that they could not cross over to us, nor we to them.

About the 29th we appeared before Tordesillas, and encamped two miles from the bridge, and about three from Rueda, which was in our rear: here we made a stand, having a good position, and a rising ground behind us. Our division encamped so regularly, that we had only to fall in, and we were ready either to fight or march. I went from this place to Olmedo with Captain Reed, our acting paymaster, to draw a fortnight's pay for the regiment. The first night we stopped at Rueda; in two days we reached Olmedo, and took up our quarters in a good house: here the captain obtained two thousand dollars, which I carried to our quarters. The next day we returned by the way of Medina del Campo, and were quartered in one of the most comfortable houses I was ever in, in this part of Spain.

The next day we reached Rueda, and were, quartered in the same house as before; and on the following morning arrived at the camp, and found things in the same state as we left them. While in this place we stripped a house and convent, not more than a mile from our camp, of all the wood. We took the roofs, door-posts, baulks, and everything that would burn, to cook with: in this part wood was uncommonly scarce. Several of the men of our division were hurt by the falling of the convent.

About the 5th of November, General Hill, with all the troops under his command, joined us at Rueda, there was a strong Spanish division also encamped about half a mile in our rear: but notwithstanding the junction of our armies, the French had the advantage both in numbers and positions. In consequence of the French Army trying to outflank us, we broke up from before Tordesillas, and fell back on Salamanca. At this period the days were fine, but the nights uncommonly cold, which greatly distressed us. In this stage of the retreat, we had plenty of provisions, but were almost destitute of clothing.

During this movement, we left Medina del Campo on our left, marched through La Nava del Rey, and moved towards Salamanca, but kept more to the right than we had ever done before: the reason of this was, that a part of the French Army was moving in this direction, in order to get into our rear, and cut off our retreat from Rodrigo; but in this they were disappointed, for we reached Salamanca in good order and in good spirits, notwithstanding our distressing marches, and took up our quarters in a convent on the north side of the city. Here we lay two days, and received orders to get whatever clothing was to be found in the general hospitals. We then obtained a seasonable supply, for many of us were nearly naked: all that I had, excepting a pair of new shoes, which were too small for me, was not worth sixpence. We had been using our present clothing almost two years, most of the time on actual service; and about five months of that period out of doors.

On the 13th November the enemy had collected in great force near the village where we had been engaged on the 20th of June. We marched to our old position, intending to give them battle; but soon returned to the convent, the enemy not daring to fight on this ground. They, however, made another attempt to turn our right flank, and to cut off our retreat: to prevent this, we took up a position on part of the same ground where the ever-memorable Battle of Salamanca, had been fought, and expected to fight another engagement to be designated the second Battle of Salamanca. The two armies were in motion, the whole of our baggage had already been sent to the rear, and our division was in line ready for battle; but the enemy still manoeuvred in order to turn our right wing, which they nearly effected, but the moment Lord Wellington learnt their intention, he gave orders for our retreat towards Rodrigo, when we broke into column, and moved off.

It now began to rain very fast, and continued all that day and most of the night: I accidentally found a biscuit-bag, and threw it over my shoulders, and every time it was saturated with water, my comrade and I wrung it out: by this means I kept much dryer than could have been expected; but after all; I was as wet as though I had been dipped in water: the rain fell in torrents, indeed, part of the country through which we passed was completely inundated. After dark, we encamped in a wood, completely drenched, and almost lost in mire and water. Here we lay in our wet clothes, exposed to the inclemency of the season, having nothing to partake of but cold water: our rum, which would have been very acceptable, could not be obtained.

After all, I got a good sleep on the wet ground until mornings when we recommenced our march. I shall ever remember these days; we marched several miles up to the ankles in water, sometimes indeed up to the knees, and continued to move along through mud and mire until night, and then encamped in a place completely flooded with water. A shrubbery being near, we cut down the boughs of the young trees, and piled them on the ground until we raised ourselves out of the water; and in this way made the best of our condition. Here we spent the night again without a morsel to eat or drink, except cold water: after all, we were cheerful, keeping up each other's spirits.

In the morning we fell in and recommenced our retreat; but had to leave one of our poor fellows, who had perished from cold and hunger: he was buried by his comrades, who with feelings of regret and sorrow consigned him to his long home.

On the 16th we moved off, it being a fine morning, and soon had to encounter the worst road I ever saw: the whole of our baggage, and part of the army, having passed along, had made it like a bog-mire. I have known some of our men sink into the mud, and stick as fast as possible; others have gone to their assistance, and all have stuck fast together! This was frequently the case: hundreds of the men lost their shoes, and were obliged to walk barefoot the remainder of the retreat. I had a strap buckled tight over each instep and under each shoe, so that I did not lose mine; but I frequently stuck fast in the mud.

We at length got out of the mire into better road; but had to quicken our pace, there being a considerable distance between us and the 5th Division, The enemy, who were on our left flank, saw and took advantage of this opening in our line of march, by dashing into it, and taking a great deal of our light baggage. Our general, Lord Dalhousie, was amongst the principal losers. At this period, General Paget, the present Marquis of Anglesey, riding to the rear to ascertain what was the cause of the 7th Division being delayed, missed his road, and was taken prisoner. The enemy pressing upon us, and our cavalry being distant, we were obliged to send the gunners of the flying artillery after them, our regiment, and the 51st moving on to their support: but the enemy scampered off at full speed with what booty they had obtained.

We at length got clear of the wood, and began to descend a steep hill, from which we had a cheering view of the British cavalry drawn up on the opposite hill: the sight was grand and encouraging to us. Having descended into the valley, we crossed a deep river, the water being as cold as ice: in a few minutes we had to cross another river, deeper than the former, and, to augment our distresses, the enemy posted themselves, with twelve pieces of cannon, on the hill from which we had just descended, and immediately commenced a desperate cannonading on our regiment and the 51st. We formed line, and stood for six hours up to the ankles in mud and water, and during that period were completely exposed, having nothing to shelter us from their fire: not a man, however, of our regiment was either killed or wounded.

When the enemy's shots came near us, we advanced two or three hundred yards, and the balls went over our heads a considerable distance; and when they shortened their quantity of powder, and the shots fell near us again, we retreated four or five hundred yards: by these means many lives were saved. I saw several branches of the trees struck off, and one horse wounded. This day we were in a miserable plight; up to the ankles in water for six hours, after a march of fifteen miles, without anything to eat or drink. After this we had to go to the brink of the river, and remain there all night, to watch the enemy, who were enjoying themselves in a village not more than half a mile distant. In an old mill, on the bank of this river, we found a poor woman lying dead; she had expired from hunger and fatigue: none of us knew who she was, but supposed her to have belonged to our army or to the Portuguese.

About midnight we received our rum, which revived us; but it made some of our men so exceedingly intoxicated, that they could not stand in the ranks. There was no wonder at this, for we had been long without food, at least forty-eight hours. About two o'clock in the morning, a regiment of light dragoons came and took our post, and we moved off to join the division, which was encamped near a wood, two miles from the river. When we reached the division, we found the wood on fire in every direction, which was unintentionally caused by the soldiers, who had made fires at the foot of the large oak trees. In this wood were a great number of pigs, which had been driven from the towns and villages in the neighbourhood to eat the acorns, and to fatten on them: scores of them were shot by our men, who thus obtained a supply of pork, but I could not procure a morsel either for love or money.

17th. We commenced our march as usual: one of our men, having a camp-kettle full of boiled wheat, gave me two or three spoons full; and this was the only food I had partaken during three whole days, so that it helped me greatly. This day I obtained leave to fall out, and coming into an enclosed country, where haws, sloes, and hips were plentiful, I stopped behind most of the day, to satisfy my craving appetite with them. We encamped in a place where wood and water were plentiful, but I was immediately ordered on the advance guard, and had to stand sentry four hours during the night. Here, to our great joy, a quantity of bread and rum reached the commissary, and we received three days' bread, and one day's meat and rum; but having had so little to eat during the last three days, my appetite was nearly gone.

I drank a little broth, and eat two small bits of biscuit, with a little meat, which seemed to go against my stomach; but in the morning my appetite came to me, and I cracked biscuits the greater part of the day. My comrade, having imprudently drank his allowance of rum upon an empty stomach, nearly lost his life in consequence: he fell asleep, and I tried every method in vain, to awake him.

At length I went to the captain, to know what was to be done: he ordered me to stop with him, and if the enemy came, I was to leave him to his fate, and make my escape to my company. When the regiment had gone out of the camp, I obtained a mule, put poor James on its back, and off we started for Rodrigo; but the sun had no sooner risen and began to warm him, than he awoke, and came to himself. We soon got sight of the city of Rodrigo, but had to cross a river called the Agueda. Up to this period I was sound and well; but in crossing this river, a quantity of sand got into my shoes, which made me a complete cripple; I had marched four of five hundred miles, and was completely knocked up. Had this happened near Salamanca, I should most certainly have been taken prisoner, as it would have been impossible for me to have got out of the way. I did not join the regiment until late in the night. We were encamped about six miles from Rodrigo, north of the Gallegos road, and not more than twelve miles from Portugal.

In the morning we marched again: I was so exceedingly lame, that I could not keep up with the regiment, but followed, and did not arrive at Alla Madilla until the evening. Indeed, I walked with the greatest pain and trouble to myself, having frequently to take off my shoes and walk barefoot. The French Army followed us until within about eight leagues of Ciudad Rodrigo, when, finding all attempts to intercept our retreat useless, they gave up further pursuit, and retired into cantonments in the neighbourhood of Salamanca. Thus, ended the memorable campaign of 1812.

CHAPTER 13

Occurrences During Winter

While at Alla Madilla, I received a letter from England, with intelligence of the death of my brother William, who had been fixed in business at Boston only eleven months, when he expired in a deep decline. The news surprised me, but being so harassed with my late sufferings during the retreat. I could not grieve, although I loved my brother, and missed him very much when I returned from Spain and Portugal. I thought it a strange and wonderful thing that I should be spared in the midst of dangers, and when near perishing with cold, fatigue, and hunger, and he be cut off from the midst of plenty, at the early age of twenty-four.

28th. This morning the colonel sent for me, saying, he was going to send me to the headquarters of the army, to be servant to a captain, who had just been transferred from the 52nd Regiment to ours: his name was Captain Charles Wood, Deputy Assistant Adjutant General. The colonel gave me a letter of recommendation, saying, he hoped I should behave well. The regiment then marched off for its winter quarters, and after a march of four days reached St. Martino, its destination. The regiment having left Alla Madilla, I started for Freynada, where I arrived about two o'clock on the same day.

The captain received me well, and ordered me to go to the other servants, who lived in the stable, where we were very comfortable and happy; indeed, after our late unparalleled sufferings and fatigues, the stable was like a palace, especially to me, who had been exposed in the open air, day and night during the summer, without a tent or covering. There were four of us lived together; myself, an English groom named Crawley, a Spanish muleteer, and a Portuguese servant: this was our family. I had to attend my master, and draw the provisions for the whole, having the Spanish muleteer to assist me in fetching the provisions from the commissary stores. My master dined with Lord

Wellington about twice a week.

Freynada, the then headquarters of the British Army, is on the frontiers of Portugal: it does not consist of more than fifty houses; has one church, and about two hundred inhabitants: it is five leagues from Rodrigo, three from Almeida; and about six from Guarda. Lord Wellington had the best house in the village; the Prince of Orange had one near the market-place; and my master's house was about one hundred yards south of the latter. Lord Wellington and his staff officers used to hunt during the winter season; and on one occasion the hounds started a large wolf, which was hunted several miles: he at length got into a hole, and thus escaped. Another day, a wild cat was started, and the hounds with difficulty succeeded in taking her. One evening a fox was brought to my master in a bag, and I was ordered to take him to the huntsman: the officers expected much sport from this fox, but were disappointed; for when he was turned out of the bag, behold, poor Reynard was already as dead as a stone.

Lord Wellington was highly respected for the inhabitants of this part of Portugal, and also by the officers and soldiers under his command. His Lordship used to walk in the market-place of Freynada for hours together, in a grey great coat, and in every respect as plainly dressed as though he had been but a captain or subaltern officer. During my stay at this place, I have often admired the affability of His Lordship. The Prince of Orange was a companion of Captain Wood's, and being a constant visitor at my master's, I had frequent opportunities of seeing him, and conversing with him. Lord Wellington has often visited our stables to view the horses, as did Lord Aylmer, and several other of the officers.

In the beginning of December, I was sent to Almeida, to procure some tarpaulins, to make my master's room more comfortable. I succeeded in obtaining some, and we divided his room. I have stated before that, in general, the houses in Spain and Portugal have no glass windows, but have large shutters instead, which are closed in winter and stormy weather. In these large shutters there is generally a small aperture left to admit the light: over this aperture we put a piece of fine cambric muslin, which answered the place of glass. We also built a fireplace and a chimney, a thing very uncommon in Portugal; and thus made his room what we called comfortable. But what a place for a nobleman's son to live in! I have seen hundreds of stables preferable to it.

On the 23rd of December I was again sent to Almeida, to purchase groceries. This is a very strong fortification, has a deep ditch, a double wall, and is in every respect well-fortified. At this period, however, there were only a few Portuguese soldiers in it. Before I got home, it became dark, and I unfortunately got into a wrong road, so that I was completely lost. However, I let the horse go his own way, and he brought me home in safety.

The next day we killed a young kid for our Christmas dinner, and we had what we considered a delightful repast, but nothing to be compared to what some of the poorest peasants have in England. However we were content, and where contentment is, there is a feast. After our dinner was over, I had to wait at table, at Lieutenant Brown's, of the adjutant general's department, where my master used to dine. We passed the evening there very comfortably.

The 5th of January being the anniversary of the taking of Rodrigo, there was to be a grand ball given by the Spaniards in honour of that memorable event. My master being invited, we left Freynada on the 4th, arrived at Allamada, and spent the evening with the 52nd Regiment: my master dined with his old companions, for he had belonged to the 52nd before he came to our regiment. After dinner, the servants and several of the Spaniards of both sexes danced what is called the *Fandango*, one of the most obscene and immodest dances: that possibly can be: they have two wooden rattles, with which they beat time: this is the favourite dance of the Spaniards and Portuguese.

The next morning, I arose at seven o'clock, and attended to my master: after breakfast, we started for the grand ball at the city of Rodrigo; arrived there about one o'clock, and was quartered in a very fine house, the lower rooms of which we used as stables. The town was all bustle, being crowded by the Spanish gentry. In the evening my master dressed, and went to the ball; but there was no feasting for me; for I was left with the baggage and horses, not having a sixpence to spend in refreshment.

Indeed, my master, neglected me very much; but I excuse him, for he was young and inexperienced. The next morning several noblemen, generals, and other officers breakfasted at our quarters, and I waited at table in my old shabby clothes. After breakfast, I and another servant set off for Guinaldo, where a ball was given by the officers of the 43rd Regiment of Light Infantry. We passed a wolf, on the road, which did not, however, show any disposition to attack us. We arrived at Guinaldo about three o'clock, and had not been long there, before my master had to dress for the ball.

While dressing, I asked him whether he thought I could travel without money or provisions; he made some frivolous excuses, and then gave me six shillings, telling me to buy some corn for the horses. The corn cost four and sixpence, so that I had only eighteen-pence for myself: I had travelled ten leagues, had been from home three days, my master not so much as asking me whether I wanted anything.

After he had gone to dine, I was invited to dine also, and got an excellent dinner, supper, and plenty of good wine. I went also to the ball, stayed until I was tired out, and then returned to my quarters, and, went to sleep; but was awoke at three o'clock in the morning to partake of refreshment and to drink wine again. After which I laid myself down, and slept on one of the forms until daylight. After breakfast we started for Freynada, and arrived there after travelling nearly sixty miles on the frontiers of Spain and Portugal.

We had a press, and every other requisite for printing, at headquarters, and all the general orders were printed. Captain Wood's employment was to sign the general orders, direct them, and send them to the different divisions, brigades, and depots under the command of Lord Wellington. I used to help to fold them up, and always carried them to the post-office. The captain, like many others, drove everything to the last push: we were all hurry and bustle until the post was ready to start.

One evening, while helping to fold up general orders, I requested the captain to give me a suit of coloured clothes, having had my present clothing more than two years, and most of that time on actual service: all the answer he made to my request was, that if I had coloured clothes the Spaniards would think nothing of me; but while I had my regimentals on, however shabby they might appear, the Spaniards would respect me; and look on me as one of their deliverers. This was an excellent excuse to save his money; but I differed in opinion with the captain, and thought a good suit of clothes would have done me infinitely more good than all the respect that might have been shown me by the Spaniards or Portuguese.

He told me, however, that I should go to the regiment, and get my new clothing. A few days after this, one of the staff officers of the sixth Division sent to headquarters for my master to accomplish a certain intrigue, which had been entered into in a Spanish family, but the thing was found out, and the servant was obliged to return without the prize. This servant had to go within one mile of our regiment, and having a spare horse, I went with him. The first day we reached Celerico, the second day I arrived at the regiment, and received my new clothing. At Celerico, on my return, I drew provisions at the

114

commissary stores; and next day I reached a small village called Subral de Sierra.

Here, for the first time in Portugal, I slept in a bed, and was very comfortable. One of the peasant's daughters said I was like her absent brother; and because of this, they were very kind to me. There was not an Englishman in the town, or near it, but myself. In the night we heard the howling of wolves: the peasant told me they would not hurt people in the daytime, but they were "*multo mal*" at night; that is, they were evil in the night. The next day I arrived at the village to which our Portuguese servant belonged. I called at his mother's, who invited me to stay all night at her house. She made a good supper for me, consisting of boiled potatoes and olive oil. I retired to rest, and slept in a corner of the room on some clean straw, having a blanket to cover me.

After partaking of a good breakfast of bread and goat's milk, I started for Freynada, and arrived there about noon. My journey was about one hundred and twenty miles, through a very romantic country: but I met with nothing but civility and the best of treatment from the Portuguese in the several towns and villages through which I passed. Indeed, at this period, I was not at a loss to know what the inhabitants said, I could speak the Portuguese language well.

In the beginning of April 1813, I was sent to the great fair at Almeida, to purchase cords, candles, and sundry other articles for my master's use. At this fair there was abundance of cords, straps, leather, salt, sugar, and everything that was requisite for necessaries or food; the fair was uncommonly crowded with buyers and sellers. Having purchased everything that I had orders for, I returned to Freynada the same evening, the captain being satisfied with what I had bought. We now began to prepare for again taking the field, and made everything ready to march at the shortest notice.

About the 10th of April, orders came for my master to leave Portugal, and to join our army in Russia, in the capacity of *aide-de-camp* to General Stewart. My master was brother to Colonel Wood, of the Royal East Middlesex Militia, and nephew, to the late Marquis of Londonderry. He said, he would take me with him to England, and from thence to Russia, and wrote the next day, requesting the colonel to place my name on the list of our depot in England. I carried the letter to the post-office with a light heart, being confident I should go with him; but all my hopes were blasted, the colonel, in answer to my master's letter, telling him, he could not allow me to leave Portugal, for it was against the standing orders of the army to allow an effective man to leave on any account. I was in consequence doomed to pass through, suffering greater than ever. The captain sold all the cordage and other necessaries that I bought at Almeida fair: he also sold two of his horses, and several other things.

On the 14th we left Freynada, in company with Mr. George Haines, brother to the assisting commissary general. We had not, however, proceeded more than six miles, when my horse ran away with me, and while in full speed, one of the stirrups broke, and I narrowly escaped being killed: but the good providence of God, in this instance as well as in many others, preserved me. I at length succeeded in stopping him, and rode back to seek my stirrup: having found it, I hung it over the peak of my saddle, and rode the remainder of the journey.

We arrived at Sabugal, and obtained the best quarters the town afforded both for ourselves, and horses. There was a visible improvement in this place: when I first passed through Sabugal, nothing could exceed the misery and distress of the inhabitants: some were dying, of hunger, and others were entirely naked. But on this occasion things seemed to smile upon them; provisions were plentiful, and tolerably cheap. The constant passing and repassing of detachments of soldiers and British officers contributed much to the improvement of this once distressed town.

During the evening I went to view the old tower, and looking from the top into a garden, I saw something like a human body, with a cord round its middle: curiosity led me to the spot, and I found it was a body which has been torn from a grave. I mentioned the circumstance to a peasant, who told me the *lobos* (that is the wolves) had done it. I left the place very ill, for the body was in a state of putrefaction.

The next day we left this place, arrived at Pedrogos about noon, and took up our quarters at the house of a druggist. I was well acquainted with this place, having been here in cantonments during the winter of 1811. In the afternoon, a party of the light division arrived here, some of whom were quartered over our stables. At night, the captain ordered me to go and sleep with the groom on the stable floor: he had some fear least the detachment should steal anything from us; indeed, his suspicions were not groundless. After securing everything, we retired early to rest; but when we awoke in the morning, to our utter astonishment we found that all our next day's provisions, a bag of horse corn, and some other things, were gone; and what was most remarkable, the things were taken from under our heads.

Indeed, such is the wretched condition of the houses in many parts of Portugal, that it is difficult to secure anything from an ingenious thief. When Captain Wood learnt that the corn was gone, he gave way to a fit of passion, and blamed me and the groom, and nothing would satisfy him but it was from our carelessness and neglect. He ordered us off to cut the standing corn, which was just coming into ear, and the horses eat it instead of the corn that had been stolen.

After breakfast, we started for Castel Branco. We had not, however, proceeded more than two miles; when I examined the baggage, and found my musket was missing. I immediately returned for it, and met my master and Mr. Haines coming out of the town. The captain enquired where I was going, and when I told him, he said if the like happened again, I should walk back. What with his scolding, the loss of our provisions, and probably my musket, I was very much confused: when I got to the door of the druggist, I called out for my musket: the woman brought it in a hurry, and was in the act of giving it to me, when the horse took fright and threw me, and the streets, being uncommonly rough, I was much injured by the fall.

I then took my musket on my shoulder, and led the horse out of the town, when I mounted and rode after the party, and soon overtook them. We arrived at Castel Branco about one o'clock, and were quartered in a very fine house at the end of a large square, where our regiment used to parade when in cantonments, in May and June, 1812. It was in this place I suffered so much from a fever, and where I sold my father's watch for four dollars, in order to procure some extra provisions and nourishment.

On the 4th day we arrived at Nisa, after passing the three villages in which I was so distressed and afflicted in the beginning of 1812; and here also I had laid seven days in a state of insensibility. We drew provisions here for ourselves and horses, and next morning started for Gaveon: after travelling half a league, we had to cross the small river, which has been mentioned in the former part of this *Narrative*. I could not help reflecting on my condition when I crossed this river at the period above-mentioned, at which time I fell in, and only just escaped with my life, and had to ride six miles in my wet clothes, and then to lay all night in them on a cold marl floor.

But on this occasion, I was mounted on a horse worth one hundred guineas, had plenty to eat and drink, and, what was still better, was in possession of good health. This day we rode over a wild country, arrived at Gaveon about mid-day, and obtained excellent stables for the horses, and good quarters for ourselves. There was an improvement in this place also; for the first time I came into this town nothing could exceed the wretched appearance of its inhabitants, but on this occasion provisions were plentiful, and there was the appearance of improvement and happiness. The next morning, we started for Abrantes, passed through, and took up our quarters at St Bertone. This is a most delightful little town: the Tagus runs past it, and vessels lay close to the doors of the houses.

I had on this march to keep a constant look out after our baggage, for some of the Portuguese are not over honest. For this purpose, I had the following list of things belonging to the captain: one bed, one portmanteau, a parcel directed to His Royal Highness the Prince of Wales, one round case of pictures for one of our nobles, whose name I have forgotten; with stable utensils, &c., &c. On the 7th day of our march, we reached Santarem, got into good quarters, and drew provisions at the commissary stores. This day my master and Mr. Haines made preparations to reach Lisbon the next day, and gave all the baggage into my charge, with directions to draw provisions at Villa Franca, and to reach Lisbon in two days; the distance being fourteen leagues.

Early the next morning we started: the captain passed us on the road, and we saw him no more until we reached Lisbon. That night we reached Villa Franca, a very good-looking town on the south bank of the Tagus. The next morning, we started, passed the strong fortified lines, and reached Lisbon about two o'clock p. m. It was sometime before we could find our master: we at length found him, and obtained excellent quarters in a gentleman's house in the north-west part of the city. I remained in Lisbon on this occasion about seven days; and being in the capacity of a servant, I had an opportunity of seeing much more of the city than I otherwise should have had.

The first day I attended Captain Wood at an inn kept by an Englishman: there was with him Captain Fitz Clarence of the 10th Light Dragoons. The next day my master went to his own quarters, and there waited for a passage to England. On this occasion I had a view of the grand church supposed to be richer than some of the churches at Rome itself. There are in Lisbon about forty churches, and fifty convents for both sexes; about twenty thousand houses, and nearly two hundred and fifty thousand inhabitants. The city is built on the side of a sloping hill, so that to those who view it from the south it has a grand effect. The streets are very filthy, and are seldom cleaned, except by the heavy rains that occasionally fall. In walking the streets of Lisbon in the summer time, I was surprised to see the quantity of flies that feed on the filth, carrion, and dirt that laid about. I questioned one of the inhabitants on the subject, who told me, they let the dirt lay in the street to keep the flies out of the houses, which would otherwise be intolerable.

There are in Lisbon several fine fountains of water, and hundreds of poor men obtain a livelihood by selling it: I have seen as many as fifty together at one fountain. There are also stationed at the corners of many of the most public streets, people who sell water and lemonade to passengers. I visited some of the wine houses, where wine was sold at about eight-pence a quart; but the stench and disagreeable smell of oil and garlic made it unpleasant for a stranger. I was at a coffee-house that was an exception to this, for everything was clean, neat, and comfortable: we had some of the best coffee I had ever tasted before.

One practice that I saw in this place was, as I thought, a very good one: the milkman came to our door, and cried, "Milk!" when I got to the door with my vessel, I saw no milk, but the man had brought his cow with him, and began to milk the quantity I wanted. The milk was pure, as he had no means or opportunity of adulterating it.

I drew provisions at the commissary stores, and as I was going home, with them, some of the inhabitants wanted to buy our beef; they offered eight *vints*, or one shilling per pound: in the shops beef was eighteen pence per pound. The next I drew at the stores was pork; few wanted to purchase it, and those that did, would only give four *vints*, or six-pence per pound.

Mr. Haines having completed his business, was ready to return to Freynada: he took with him eighteen couples of hounds for his brother, and a young grey stallion, which had cost about two hundred guineas. Mr. Haines, wanted a man to ride this horse, and to follow the hounds up the country. Captain Wood gave me my wages, with a letter to Colonel Johnson, telling me at the same time I must go with Mr. Haines and assist him up to headquarters, and then join my regiment. For this purpose, I joined Mr. Haines and suite in the capacity of groom and whipper-in to his hounds: there were besides two English soldiers, a Spaniard, and a Portuguese servant.

On Wednesday the 28th April we commenced our march up the country; but I had the greatest difficulty in managing the young stallion: he had never been properly broken in; besides, I had only a common snaffle bridle, so that he was often unmanageable, and very restive. We had only got two leagues, when I had like to have lost my life in ascending a hill. Meeting a party of the royal waggon-train, I and my horse got on the wrong side: the drivers would not stop; my horse reared up, and fell backwards, in the fall I was severely hurt, and could not mount for some time. As we were walking along, the horse made a spring at me, and I was obliged to let him go; but he was stopped by two peasants.

Our Portuguese servant coming up, took him and galloped several times across the fields: by this time, I had recovered from the effects of my fall, and he carried me the remainder of the journey as quiet as possible. We reached Villa Franca about three o'clock, and on the 30th Santarem.

May 1st. We arrived at Golgon. The 10th Light Dragoons being in this town, Mr. Haines accommodated the officers with his hounds, but they found little diversion here. I and the other servants moved off for Punhetta, and Mr. Haines joined us on the road. We arrived at the above-mentioned place, and took up our quarters in a very good house.

May 3rd. We arrived at Abrantes, rode through the city, crossed the River Tagus, and were quartered on the south side, amongst the stores; for on this spot stood the grand magazine for the armies. There were many thousand bags of biscuit and rice, barrels of rum, and a great quantity of military stores of every description.

4th. We left this delightful place, but we had not proceeded more than six miles, when Mr. Haines told me to get off, and flog one of the dogs, which I accordingly did: but letting go my hold of the horse, he set off at full gallop. I ran after him, expecting he would not have stopped until he had reached the stables where he had been during the last night: he was stopped, however, in a village about two miles distant. I gave the peasants a quart of wine for their trouble, and then made the horse go back for my pleasure.

Having overtaken Mr. Haines, we proceeded on our journey to Gaveon, but were so troubled with the large gad flies, that infest this country, that the horses could scarcely travel: the road being rough, and the stallion not used to it, he was awkward, and stumbled very much; but we arrived at Gaveon without an accident, and obtained the same stables that we had before. On this day's march we passed through a wood of cork-trees, of the bark of which the inhabitants make several useful utensils; the corks we use in this country are nothing but the bark of these trees. The Portuguese in this and other parts of Portugal make their milking vessels of it.

5th. We left Gaveon, and arrived at Nisa, where we obtained excellent quarters. 6th. We reached Castel Branco: this was the fifth time I had been in this city. 7th. We started for Pedrogos: this day we had a deal of trouble with the dogs, for the country abounded with hares, rabbits, and foxes, so that the hounds frequently started off in full cry, and it was very difficult to flog them off. When we got within a league of Pedrogos, a large fox ran across the road; the dogs saw him, and followed: Mr. Haines called for me to flog them off, but my horse going so fast, I had enough to do to keep on the saddle, especially on this occasion, for my horse leaped over several large heaps of stones and deep ditches, and what made it more difficult, we had a very steep hill to descend. At last, we succeeded in getting the dogs off, and no accident happened to us, more than a few of the couples being broken. We arrived at Pedrogos, received provisions at the stores, and the next morning set off for Sabugal, which we reached about noon; and the next day, after a pleasant journey, arrived in safety at Freynada.

Map of the
SPANISH CAMPAIGN.

English Miles

0 20 40 60 80 100   200

CHAPTER 14

Opening of the Campaign of 1813

Everything was now in readiness for the opening of the projected campaign. Lord Wellington had, during the time our army was in cantonments, used every exertion for getting, it into the best possible state of equipment and discipline, and he commenced operations with the determination of deciding at once, by vigorous measures, the fate of the Peninsula; and as the Allied Army had been considerably augmented by large reinforcements from England, as well as by numerous Portuguese levies, he found himself enabled to act agreeably to his wishes. The force under his command consisted of fifty-four thousand seven hundred British, and thirty-four thousand four hundred Portuguese troops, as I myself saw in the statement given in by Lieutenant Brown, Deputy Assistant Adjutant-General, to Lord Wellington.

Of these, about nine thousand might be sick; so that there was left an efficient army of eighty thousand excellent soldiers, in high health and spirits, eager for combat, and looking forward to victory and conquest. The French, in the meantime, well knowing the quality of the troops, and the skill and activity of the commander with whom they had to contend, concentrated without delay their forces in the neighbourhood of Burgos, and there awaited with boldness the advance of the British chief.

Towards the middle of May, 1813, our army, which had been joined by about twenty thousand Spaniards, broke up from their winter quarters, and marched in three columns in quest of the enemy. The first column, under Sir Rowland Hill, had received orders to proceed by Toledo; the centre column, or main body of the army, under the immediate command of Lord Wellington, advanced to Salamanca; and the third, or left column, commanded by Sir Thomas Graham, was to move across the Douro, through Miranda, to the banks of the Esla. To the last-mentioned column our division was attached. The different columns were to unite near Valladolid, in order to force the enemy's position near Burgos, and drive them beyond the Ebro.

Every man had now to join his respective regiment: accordingly, on the 12th May, after receiving a route, and three days' provisions, I left Freynada, the headquarters of the British Army, in order to join my regiment, then lying at St. Martino, about thirty-two miles from Celerico, on the Coimbra road; and on the 15th I reached Celerico. On entering the town, I heard the sound of bugles, and thought it was a regiment marching through; in this I was right, for the 68th, 51st, and 82nd Regiments had passed through on their way to Trancosa, where the campaign opened with the 7th Division.

I immediately reported myself to the *commandant*, who ordered me three days' provisions. After receiving them, and resting until about four o'clock in the afternoon, I set off in company with some men of our regiment. During this journey, we passed over a mountain that was at least five miles across, and joined the regiment at eleven o'clock at night in a camp at Trancosa; The next morning I saw the colonel, and gave him the letter from Captain Wood: he was pleased to see me again, and asked me several questions concerning the captain. My old companion James Mann being here, I divided the contents of my purse with him, amounting to four dollars.

16th. We marched to Castel Rodrigo, and encamped: here Captain Reed gave me a guinea in part of my pay, having received no money since November 1812. Next day we marched to Villa Nova, and on the 19th reached the south bank of the Douro, and prepared to cross it. This part of the river is broad, and the current runs very strong; we embarked by companies in clumsy boats, and after the whole had passed over, we marched up a very steep mountain, the zig-zag ascent of which was nearly five miles, and encamped at the top of it, near a good looking town called Villa Toro, on the road leaching to Miranda.

20th. We moved off left in front towards Miranda, but encamped five miles to the north of that city. We lay five days in this camp, and were reviewed by Lieutenant-General Graham, and on the following day by Lieutenant-General the Earl of Dalhousie, the commander of our division, which at this time consisted of the following regiments: 51st, 68th, 82nd, the Chasseurs Britanniques, three regiments of Portuguese infantry, and a German brigade consisting of three regiments. There were three brigades composing the 7th Division, in all ten regiments, also a brigade of heavy artillery, making a total of about eight thousand men.

26th. We marched about fifteen miles, and encamped on the top of a high hill. Here it was reported that the enemy was very near us.

27th. Early this morning the division was in motion, and marched to a small village only seven miles from the fords of the Esla, a large river which is a branch of the Douro, and there waited until Lord Wellington and his staff joined us. Here we halted until the 30th, and washed our clothes. This day I was on the brigade guards and saw some curious tricks played off by our soldiers upon the bakers of this small town. Several of them went into a bake-house, under the pretence of buying bread: each getting hold of a loaf, they ran off in different directions, and the baker after them, crying "Stop thief!" Being on sentry near the spot, I ran after the bread-stealers, without having the least intention of catching them, knowing myself what it was to be hungry and scarce of provisions.

On the evening of the 29th, orders were received for our division to march at half-past two o'clock in the morning; but the 51st Regiment was to move off precisely at twelve o'clock, in order to ford the Esla, and to dislodge the enemy from the opposite bank. Accordingly, at twelve they marched; at two the bugles of our regiment sounded, and at half-past we moved off left in front, and arrived at the fording place about five. We there saw a most distressing sight; the current ran so exceedingly strong, that it took several men off their feet, and they were immediately buried in the water.

The 51st Regiment had some of their men drowned, and several muskets and black caps were lost in the river. Many men of other regiments also were almost drowned. When we were drawn up on the bank of the river, I saw several Portuguese soldiers struggling in the water. A number of heavy dragoons were then stationed with ropes, in order to assist the men in fording the river; but notwithstanding all the assistance that was or could be given, several men lost their lives, others their muskets and caps, and were very much distressed.

Our regiment had no sooner reached the fording place, than we began to prepare to cross. Taking off our pouches, and placing them on the top of our knapsacks, we waited the word of command, confidently expecting that in a few minutes some of us should meet with a watery grave; but while we were thus contemplating our perilous condition, and expecting the worst of consequences, orders came that not any more of the troops were to cross the fords, but were to march to the pontoon bridge that by this time was ready for the army to cross the river.

Nothing could exceed the joy we felt in this sudden change in our prospects, for the order relieved us from some of the most painful and uncomfortable fears. We immediately righted our pouches, and moved towards the pontoon bridge, which was made of large tin boats, that were moored about five feet from each other: strong spars were laid from one boat to the other, and then planked over with thick planks. I had often seen these boats upon waggons travelling with us, little thinking they were so essentially useful, for with these we could have crossed any river in Spain, however formidable, with the greatest ease.

The boat bridges in Portugal are made on the same principle. Our division marched over the bridge; it sprung very much; but the whole army, with cavalry, artillery, ammunition, baggage, and everything that belonged to them, passed over, I believe, without an accident. We continued our march about five miles further, and encamped on a delightful green, near a small village, and piled our arms. The wood and watering parties had already been sent out; the foraging party, to which I belonged, were employed in cutting forage; when, suddenly, the bugle sounded the alarm, and every man ran to his arms. It was reported that the French were only one mile from us, and rapidly advancing upon our division. That we might be the better prepared for them, we immediately advanced to the top of the hill in our front, formed line, and waited for them; but on this occasion no enemy appeared; for instead of advancing on us, they had retreated toward Zamora. In consequence of this, we returned to the green, and pitched our tents: each company had three tents, and a mule to carry them.

31st. The bugle sounded as usual, and we marched towards Zamora: but instead of going direct, we kept about three miles to the left of that city, and encamped in a plain, where wood was extremely scarce, and the greatest difficulty was experienced in cooking. I travelled at least four miles, to procure sticks to cook my provisions.

On the 1st June we moved off in the direction of Toro, and during the day started several fine hares, some of which were caught by the major's dogs. After marching over a very level and pleasant country, we encamped by the road side, about three miles from the city of Toro, and close to the River Douro. Being encamped in a beautiful meadow, our situation was tolerably comfortable.

2nd. We took the direction of Toro, and in a little time passed the walls of that city: its appearance was gothic. I only passed by the town, so that I can say little concerning it. On a plain, between Toro and Tordesillas, we were reviewed by Lord Wellington. At this review there were two divisions: the 6th Division formed the first line, and the 7th the second; in all about sixteen thousand men. Being on the line of march, the two divisions were ordered into line, with their right flanks resting on the main road: His Lordship came in front of the 6th Division, attended by the following distinguished officers: the Prince of Orange, Marshal Beresford, the Commander in Chief of the Portuguese Army. Colonel Gordon, Captain Freemantle, Lord Aylmer, Quartermaster-General Murray, Colonel de Lancy, and several other officers of rank. The reason I mention so many of these names is, because I was with them at Freynada during the winter.

As soon as Lord Wellington had rode along the front and up the rear of the 6th Division, he immediately came in front of ours. Lieutenant-General the Earl of Dalhousie gave the word of command, to the brigadiers for a general salute: he and all the other generals in the division were uncovered daring the time that the bands of the different regiments were playing the national air of "God save the King." After which, the commander in chief rode along the front and up the rear of the division: we then advanced in line, and after marching about three miles, broke into open column, and marched past His Lordship and staff officers, each company saluting as they passed by. After His Lordship was satisfied with our manoeuvres, he ordered us to proceed to our encampment.

On our way thither, we passed several dead men and horses, that had been killed in a skirmish with the enemy's rearguard, in which affray about twenty thousand rations of bread fell into our hands. We encamped about eight miles from Tordesillas, in a wild country, where not a single house or even hovel or barn was to be seen from our camp. The next morning, we moved in the direction of the above city, but after marching three miles, we took another direction, leaving it on our right hand, and encamped in a meadow to the left of the main road. Here water was plentiful, but bad; and wood was so extremely scarce, that it was with difficulty we obtained fires to cook, our provisions.

Notwithstanding these privations, we on the whole passed a pleasant night, and were much refreshed. Early on the following morning we marched through a village, and were very much delighted with some of the Spaniards, who danced the *fandango*, and others of them shouted "Long live the English!" This day we marched through several villages: the bells rang, the peasants shouted, and there was nothing but joy and gladness, and the best of feelings manifested towards us by the Spanish peasantry. In the evening we encamped near Valladolid, and sent several of our sick men to the hospital of that place.

During the night one of our poor men died, and in the morning, we buried him under a tree; we then marched towards Palencia, and encamped at the foot of a very high hill, on the top of which stands a gothic village. Early the next morning we ascended the hill, marched full east through woods and plains, over hills and through valleys, for nearly twenty-six miles, and encamped at a small village situated on a branch of the Douro, five miles south of the above city. Here the enemy had blown up the bridge. There was wood in abundance on the other side of the river; and in order that we might obtain a supply of an article so essential, we swam over, and having thrown the wood into the water, jumped in after it, and pushed it before us, by these means we soon obtained excellent fires, and were very comfortable.

The next morning, we marched through Palencia, and after continuing our route twelve miles further, encamped in a complete wilderness. At this time, we were near the enemy, and confidently expected that an engagement would soon take place. About the 8th June we began to be exceedingly scarce of provisions; the army advanced so fast, that our supplies could not keep up with us, and we began to suffer much.

10th. We left this wilderness, and it being a rainy day, we were completely drenched. In the afternoon we encamped in a kind of swamp, and were obliged to gather sticks to lay at the bottom of our tents, to raise us out of the water. In the streets betwixt the tents, it was ankle deep with mire and water, but with a deal of labour and trouble we contrived to raise ourselves out of it, and slept comfortably, all things considered. The commander in chief, and his staff, were quartered in a small walled town two miles from our camp ground. My comrade having been there, brought with him about six pounds of flour, which he had taken from a peasant: this was a valuable prize to us, who were nearly famished for the want of bread; it was of more value to us at this time than gold or silver.

The next morning, we marched out of the mud and mire, and the day being fine, the roads were soon dry: after marching the usual distance, we encamped near a very pleasant river, and had a comfortable night's rest; but still wanted bread. Some days each man received two pounds of beef, and on other occasions was served out with four ounces of rice. We were in this predicament for ten or twelve days. I verily believe I did not receive more than three pounds of bread or biscuit for twelve days.

About this time, I mounted the commissary's guard, and was placed sentinel over some mouldy bread: an officer, who felt the keen and painful sensations of hunger, came to my post to steal a loaf, but I kept such a good look out that he found it very difficult to obtain one: at length he actually took it from before my face. I reproved him for his conduct, but such was his reply, that I let him go with what he had obtained. After he had gone, I took some of the bread myself, but, notwithstanding my hunger, I could not eat it by reason of its bitterness;

On the 13th we were in the neighbourhood of Burgos, but our division kept about eighteen or twenty miles to the north of that fortress. In a few hours; however, we heard that the enemy had blown up the inner walls of the castle with so little skill, that thirty men of the garrison perished by the explosion. The garrison of Burgos joined the army to which they belonged, and it was said that the whole of the French were retreating as fast as possible upon Vittoria, leaving all their strong positions uncontested. Such now was the rapidity of our movements, that we made no halts, and I had no means of learning the names of the cities, towns, and villages through which we were led by our gallant commander, especially as we encamped at a distance from them.

At this period our condition from want of provisions was miserable in the extreme: there were none to be bought for money. I have known hundreds of our men eat bean-tops, or any green herb that could be eaten. Every day after the army had encamped, and when the bullocks were killed, it was a common practice with us to catch the blood, which we boiled until quite sad, and this served as a substitute for bread. I have known twenty or thirty men, as soon as the butcher had made the incision, rush forward to obtain a supply. It was laughable to see soldiers falling one over the other, some of them covered with blood. I knew one man, during this famine, who was so exceedingly hungry, that he eat the raw tripe in its dirty state: indeed, some of the Chasseurs Britanniques used to boil the bullocks' hides until tender, and eat them.

On the 15th we were in the neighbourhood of the Ebro, and on the 16th crossed it without opposition, and marched in the direction of Vittoria. After we had encamped, I was sent on the commissary guard; but such was the scarcity of breads that the duty of guard was merely a nominal one, for we had nothing to protect, except the deputy assistant commissary: we went through all the formalities, placing a sentinel over his tent, and relieving him every two hours. Here again we had no bread, but received two pounds of beef, or rather carrion; for I am sure the people in England would not have eaten it: I never saw anything to equal it before.

The next morning, we marched with the commissary's baggage: he had a few loaves of bread, which were in charge of some Portuguese soldiers. In ascending a very steep hill, we came to a hedge full of crabs, and such was our eagerness to obtain food, that we began to eat them with as much avidity as though they had been the most delicious food. We at length proceeded on our march, but had not gone far, before we discovered that one of the Portuguese soldiers was stealing some of the loaves. I caught him in the very act, and mentioning the circumstance to my comrades, we held a sort of council, and made a prisoner of him, telling him, he should be reported to the commissary.

He said, if we would not report him, he would divide a loaf amongst us: to this offer we agreed, and immediately sat down and divided the bread. After eating it, we proceeded on our journey, but the small piece of bread which I had eaten made me so hungry, that I knew not what to do with myself.

After marching two miles, we made a proposal to the corporal of the guard, that if he would allow us to strike off from the line of march two or three, miles, to endeavour to obtain some provisions, he should have a share of whatever we might obtain. There were four of us in this party, two of whom were named Lee and Jones. Off we started in search of something to eat, and were determined to have it if in the country. We had only proceeded two miles, when we discovered a village, which we entered; and we immediately saw some young kids running loose in the streets.

I was for making sure of one of them, but was stopped by Lee, who said he would have something better. We immediately entered one of the houses, where all was ruin and desolation: the furniture broken, the inhabitants fled, and nothing to be seen like victuals, except some bacon swarth, which I seized, and eat with greediness. We left this house of misery, and came to another that was inhabited: the man, his wife, and children, were at the door crying; they told us that the French had taken all the bread and flour out of the village: this we did not believe; and notwithstanding the cry and entreaty of the family, we entered the house, and began to search for their hidden treasures of provisions.

Having obtained a quantity of Indian corn and wheat, I left the room, being highly delighted with my prize. We then collected in front of the house, and demanded of the peasant, in strong terms, a supply of provisions, telling him of our wants: he would not, however, give us a morsel of bread, or a handful of flour. At this time a Portuguese soldier, who had just joined our party, stepped up to me, and said that the peasant had got one of my comrades in the stable, and that he would surely kill him with his knife. On hearing this, we found that Lee was missing. I and the Portuguese soldiers went immediately to the stable door, and with our muskets forced it open: we learnt that Lee had promised, if the Spaniard would only give him some flour, he would decoy us off.

The moment we entered the stable, one of the men seized the sack of flour with an intent to carry it off; in the struggle my bayonet fell out of its scabbard, the Spaniard seized it, and had his hand lifted up to run me through, but the Portuguese soldier knocked him backwards, and Jones, being a strong man, seized the bag, and bore it away in triumph. We could not have rejoiced more if it had been a bag of diamonds. After carrying it completely out of the town, we divided to each man his proper share. I got about fifteen pounds, but Lee had no share with us, for we considered him unfaithful, and not worth our notice.

After dividing, the spoil, we left this part as quickly as possible, and reaching the main road, proceeded on the line of march. I could not help reflecting on the misery and horrors of war: it was hunger, and that alone, that drove many of us frequently to take what was not our own. Had we been found out, we should have been severely punished; for our commanders were very strict in protecting the Spaniards against outrages of this sort. But hunger is a sharp thorn, and few would have acted otherwise.

We shortly came to a village, and making a fire; cooked some flour and water, but had not a grain of salt amongst us. The first man that came by fortunately had some, and as he gave us a little, we invited him to partake of our repast. Nothing could exceed the misery of this village: not a single eatable was to be found in it; the straggling soldiers had even robbed the bees of their honey, and had killed nearly every fowl that could be found. I ran a great distance after one, but could not catch it. After partaking of our flour and water, and resting one hour, we proceeded on our march.

When we had marched about six miles, we sat down to rest by the side of a beautiful spring of water: a brigade of mules passing at the time, one of our party got a loaf of bread, and shared it amongst us. At this time a poor woman belonging to the army came by, and in a most affecting manner begged for a morsel of bread, saying, she had not eaten any for three days: but such was the scarcity of that valuable article, that we could not spare her one morsel, not knowing when we should get another supply. Some may think it strange that we did not relieve this poor woman's necessity; but it will not appear so when it is considered that the loaf weighed only three pounds, and there were six hungry men to partake of it: besides, there were hundreds on the same road in her situation; indeed, at this crisis, it was every man for himself, as it invariably is in time of famine.

After eating our bread, and drinking a portion of this sweet and refreshing water, we proceeded on our march, passed through another village, and saw several grievous and heartrending scenes amongst the famishing soldiers and their wives. We arrived at the camp of our division about eight o'clock at night, and joined our respective companies. It was my wish to share the flour with my comrade, but he was on the brigade guard. After supper, I laid down in the tent, put the flour under my head, and slept soundly until morning, but when I awoke, to my great grief my flour was all gone, except about a quart. I verily believe, if I had found out the thief, I should have killed him if possible, for I had risked my life for the flour, and to lose it in this way seemed to one at that time a hard case.

The next morning, we marched again, and arrived at a plain and open country, and there encamped in a pleasant situation. When my comrade joined me, he had only a small share of the flour I intended for him and myself to enjoy together.

19th. This day we marched about eighteen miles, and heard that the enemy was at no great distance.

20th. We moved off again, and I obtained liberty to leave the ranks for a short time. I called at the house of a peasant, situated near the road, and begged of him to give me a little bread or flour: he, in a very feeling manner, gave me about a quarter of a pound of flour, and said, he would have given me more had it been in his power. This day we encamped about sixteen miles from Vittoria, and our commissary served out to the brigade a mixture of wheat, barley, rye, oats, and straw. We were now put on a level with the horses and mules, for they had the same sort of provisions; but neither the horses nor the mules could eat their corn with greater eagerness than we eat ours. My comrade and I sorted our grain, and then rubbed it between two stones: it thickened our soup, and made it more nourishing—The two armies were now in sight of each other.

On the morning of the 21st June, we moved in the direction of Vittoria. We did not march by the direct road, but crossed the country, and climbed several hills that were almost inaccessible, and descended others that were very dangerous by reason of their steepness. At length we got clear of these hills, and after a short halt prepared to take an active part in the celebrated battle of Vittoria, which had already commenced.

CHAPTER 15

Splendid Engagement at Vittoria

On the night of the 19th, the enemy had taken a position, with his left resting upon the heights which end at Puebla de Arlanzon, and extended from thence across the valley of Zadora, in front of the village of Arunez. This position was covered along its front by the River Zadora, which was not anywhere fordable at this period of the year. On the 21st, the operations commenced with the occupation of the enemy's post on the heights of La Puebla, by the second Division, under the command of Sir Rowland Hill. The enemy, aware of the importance of this post, sent successively strong reinforcements for maintaining it; while, on the other hand, detachment after detachment of British troops were ordered to the attack, and a severe conflict ensued, which ended in the allies obtaining possession of the heights.

Sir Rowland Hill afterwards successfully passed the Zadora, at La Puebla, and the defile formed by the heights and the river, and attacked and gained possession of the village of Sabijana de Alava, in front of the hostile line. The enemy made many, fruitiest attempts to recover their loss. The fourth and light divisions passed the Zadora immediately after General Hill had obtained possession of the above-mentioned village. The third, division, under General Picton, crossed the bridge above Mendonza, and was followed by our division, under the Earl of Dalhousie. These four divisions were destined to attack the heights, on which the right of the enemy's centre was placed; whilst General Hill moved forward from Sabijana de Alava to attack the left.

The Third Division having taken their position, we moved along their rear; but such was the fierceness of the enemy's fire, that we had to run in double quick time past the rear of the Fifth Regiment of Foot, whose colours were unfurled, and they were ready to dash upon the enemy when the signal should be given for that purpose. Having arrived at our station and taken our position on the right of General

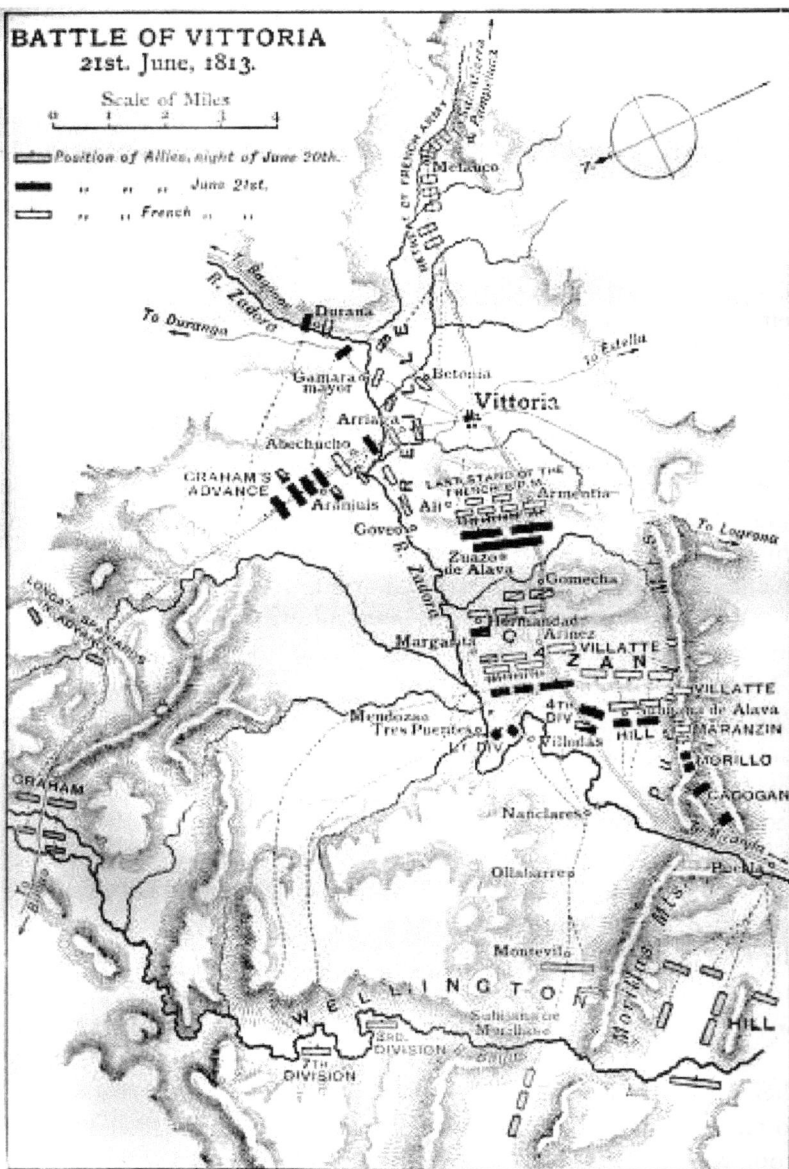

BATTLE OF VITTORIA
21st. June, 1813.

Scale of Miles

0   1   2   3   4

▭▭▭ *Position of Allies, night of June 20th.*

▬▬▬   „   „   „   *June 21st.*

▭▭▭   „   „   „   *French   „   „*

To Duranga

R. Bayas

R. Zadorra

Durana

Metauco

LINE OF FRENCH RETREAT

R. Pampluna

Gamara mayor

Betoria

To Estella

Arriaga

Vittoria

Abechucho

GRAHAM'S ADVANCE

Arinaiz

Ali

LAST STAND OF THE FRENCH 6 P.M.

Armentia

To Logrona

Goveoo

Zuazo de Alava

Gomecha

Margarita

Hermandad

Arinez

VILLATTE

ZAN

VILLATTE

Mendozao

Tres Puentes

4TH DIV.

Subijana de Alava

MARANZIN

1ST DIV

Villodas

HILL

MORILLO

CADOGAN

GRAHAM

Nanclares

Ollabarreo

Puebla

Montevito

Mogilbos Mts.

WELLINGTON

Subijana de Morillas

HILL

7TH DIVISION

3RD DIVISION

Picton's division, we waited for further orders.

This day, it was my turn to carry the camp-kettle of the mess; but it having no bottom, I requested Captain Reed to allow me to throw it away: after much hesitation he gave me leave. I immediately threw it away, pleased enough to get rid of such a piece of useless lumber. The 7th Division being now ready to advance, Lord Dalhousie ordered our brigade to move to the summit of the hill. "There, my lads," said the general, "show yourselves to the enemy!"

The signal being given, we advanced in line under cover of our brigade of nine-pounders, which continued playing over our heads until they had like to have killed some of the Portuguese skirmishers on our left. The signal was then given for them to cease firing, and to advance after the division. I don't know that I ever saw the 68th Regiment march better in line than they did into the Battle of Vittoria: every man was as steady as possible. We continued to advance until we reached a small wood: we then received a galling fire from the enemy. One of our company, named Taylor, received a severe wound, and several others fell dead at our feet. As I was loading my piece, a shot came and broke the ramrod in my hand: I changed my musket immediately with a wounded man, and took my place on the right of the rear rank of my company.

On the other side of the wood, there was a division of the enemy's infantry drawn up ready to receive us, and when we came within a short distance, they poured a volley upon us which did great execution, wounding Colonel Johnson in two places and killing several of the men. We continued to advance until we had got through the wood, when the firing from the enemy became dreadful, and our men fell in every direction. I really thought that, if it lasted much longer, there would not have been a man left to relate the circumstances. We now came to plain ground, and continued to move forward, while the French infantry retreated before us.

We then came to a certain height, where the enemy had twelve pieces of cannon placed, with which they opened a most destructive fire upon us; our brigade-major's horse had both his forelegs shot from under him; the poor creature began to eat grass, as if nothing was the matter with him. We still advanced towards the enemy's battery, but were so weakened by their fire, that we were obliged to take shelter in a deep ditch, not more than two hundred yards from the muzzles of their guns. In that part of the ditch where I was, the brigade-major had taken shelter. It was now reported by some of our timid soldiers

Battle of Vittoria, June 21, 1813

that the enemy was advancing, and that we should all be taken prisoners; but, resolving to avoid being taken, if possible, I looked up to see whether the enemy was advancing or not. I had scarcely raised my head above the ditch, when a grapeshot struck the top of my cap, and carried away the rosette, with part of the crown: had it been three inches lower, I should have been no more. "There, Green," said one of our men, "it has only just missed your head!"

I observed to the brigade-major that it was sharp work; "aye," said he; "yet we are well off, if we can only keep so." He had scarcely uttered these words, however, when our company was ordered to the left to skirmish, and such was the quickness of the enemy's fire; that we were obliged to get out of the ditch one by one, and run squatting along to our station. We then opened a brisk fire upon the enemy, which continued several minutes. It appeared that we had advanced about fifteen minutes too soon for the light division, which was to have supported us; at length this division came in sight: our regiment and brigade immediately sprang over the ditch, gave three cheers, and charged the enemy, the light division breaking their ranks in haste to join us.

We then mingled our shouts together, and dashed forward against the foe. It was grand to see the divisions striving to outdo each other in gallantry. The enemy could not withstand the shock, but were panic-struck, and fled in confusion: we followed them, shouting and huzzaing, and gave them no time to form, but drove them before us like cattle to destruction. In the meantime, Sir Thomas Graham, who commanded the left of the army, moved forward towards Vittoria, by the high road from that town to Bilboa. The enemy had a division of infantry and some cavalry advanced on this road, resting their right on some strong height covering the village of Gamarra Major: the height and village, however, were soon carried, and the defeat of the enemy was now complete.

Nothing could exceed the joy we felt, to see the enemy flying before us in dismay and confusion. After driving them through Vittoria, our division encamped within two miles of that city: the cavalry and a part of the infantry followed them several miles, and harassed their rearguard. The rolls were called over, and we found that the total loss of the 68th Regiment in this memorable battle was as follows: Colonel Johnson, wounded in the body and arm; Captain Anderson and Lieutenant Perwin, killed, Captains Gough, Reed, and Irwin, Lieutenants Hinds, Balls, M'Coy, and Shean, and Sergeant-Major Kearns,

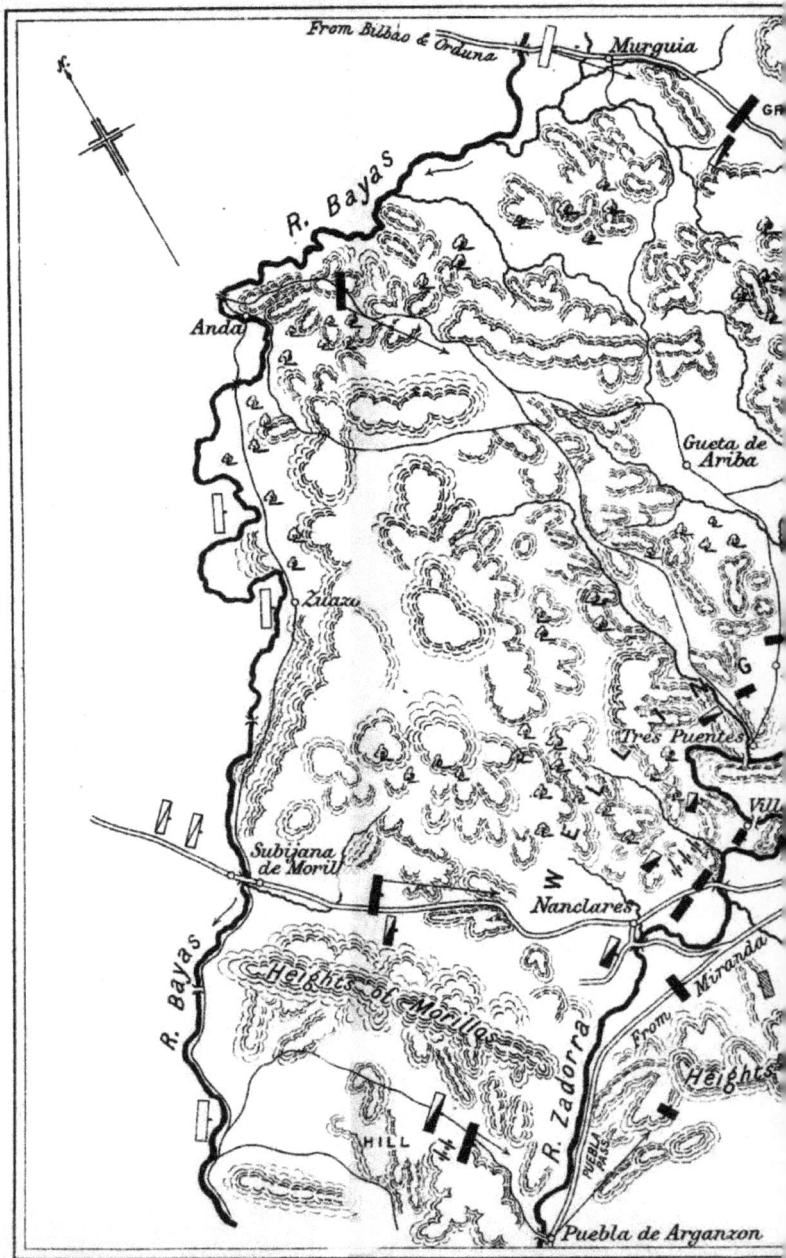

From Bilbáo & Orduna — Murguia

GR

R. Bayas

Anda

Gueta de
Ariba

Zuazo

G

Tres Puentes

Vill

Subijana
de Moril

Nanclares

Heights of Morillos

R. Bayas

R. Zadorra

From Miranda

Heights

HILL

PUEBLA
PASS

Puebla de Arganzon

BATTLE OF
VITTORIA
21ˢᵗ June 1813.

The general character of the ground between the Zadorra and the Bayas was broken and wooded, hilly and intersected by many streams.

From Bilbao and Orduña

Durana

Gamarra
Menor

Gamarra
Mayor

Abechuco

To Bayonne

R. Zadorra

Ariaga

Betonio

Ali

French Position

Baggage
Waggons

To Pampeluna

Last French Position

Vittoria

Line of French Retreat

Margarita

Hermandad

Zu. xo. de
Alava

Arinez

Gomecha

Armentia

Subijana
de Alava

of Puebla

Allies............ ▬▬
French............ ▬▬
Position of Allies on the 20ᵗʰ June...... ▭

ENGLISH MILES

0   ½   1   2   3

Stanford's Geogˡ Estabˡ, London.

wounded; and one hundred and seventy non-commissioned officers and privates killed and wounded.

At the commencement of the action, our regiment did not consist of more than three hundred and fifty effective men in the field, so that our loss was very great; perhaps equal to any regiment in the army consisting of the same number of men. The wife of Joseph Buonaparte was taken prisoner in her carriage, and Joseph himself narrowly escaped the same fate. The commander in chief, however, gave orders that she should be escorted by ten light dragoons into the French lines. Several men of our regiment obtained a great deal of money: one, named Sullivan, found one thousand dollars amongst the baggage of the enemy: another, called Kenneville, who now lives at Scotton near Lincoln, obtained one hundred and eighty *doubloons*, which are equal to sixteen dollars each, amounting in all to seven hundred and twenty pounds sterling.

Others of the men found valuable clothing: in short, the whole of the baggage of the enemy, together with their treasury, fell into our hands. A gown-piece, some children's frocks, two flutes, an English bible, and a few other small articles, were all that fell to my share. I fancy someone had had the bible in his possession who, could not carry all his treasure, and therefore threw it aside, in order to make room for what he considered to be of more value.

The loss of the Allies in this action was great, amounting to nearly five thousand men in killed, wounded, and missing. The particulars are as follows: one lieutenant-colonel, nine captains, eleven lieutenants, seven ensigns, and one staff-officer, killed; one general staff-officer, eight lieutenant-colonels, nine majors, fifty-six captains, one hundred and seven lieutenants, forty-one ensigns, and nine staff-officers, wounded; six hundred and twenty-two non-commissioned officers and privates, and ninety-three horses, killed; three thousand four hundred and eighty-seven men, and seventy-six horses, wounded.

The Spaniards had ninety-eight men killed, and four hundred and sixty-three wounded. The total loss, therefore, of the Allied Army, was seven hundred and forty men killed, and four thousand one hundred and eighty-one wounded; making a grand total in killed, wounded, &c., four thousand nine hundred and twenty-one.

The loss of the enemy, in killed, wounded, and missing, was about sixteen thousand men. There were also taken one hundred and fifty pieces of cannon, four hundred and fifteen ammunition waggons, containing fourteen thousand two hundred and forty-nine rounds of ammunition for guns and howitzers; one million nine hundred and seventy-three thousand and four hundred musket-ball cartridges, forty thousand six hundred and sixty-eight pounds of gunpowder, fifty-six forage waggons, and forty-eight forge waggons; including, in fact, the whole *matériel* of the French Army.

Lord Wellington passed very high encomiums on the British Army: in his despatches, he says, "I cannot too highly extol the conduct of both officers and men." He remarked also, that it was impossible for the movements of any troops to be conducted with more spirit and regularity than those of the respective divisions of Sir Rowland Hill, the Earl of Dalhousie, Sir Thomas Picton, Sir Lowry Cole, and Major-General Alten.

After the engagement, I was sent to a small village near Vittoria, to remain with one of our men, who was taken very ill. I and several other men went into a house to obtain plunder: in a room upstairs stood a desk, and several of the soldiers were in the act of forcing it open to get possession of its supposed valuable contents. No sooner was the lid forced open, then every eye was fixed, and every hand ready to seize the treasure: after searching for some time, out came a paper parcel full of what resembled *doubloons*: every man made a grasp at it, thinking to gain the golden prize; when it turned out to be a parcel of gilt buttons!

We were much confused at this, and it was really ludicrous to see the disappointment of the soldiers. I immediately went into another house, and there obtained a quantity of dough, and made for myself and sick companion a comfortable mess, having previously obtained some flesh meat in the French camp. Previous to this, and immediately after the engagement, I met with a townsman, named Kirk, of the 3rd or King's Own Dragoons, who gave me a piece of bread, which was very acceptable. After this I made an attempt to obtain provisions at a gentleman's house: the peasant who was on the spot was an intelligent man; he was overjoyed at our successes, and relieved my wants to the extent of his ability.

Early on the morning of the 22nd, I and my sick companion joined the regiment, and found many of our men so exceedingly rich, that they could not carry their load of treasures. My comrade had got a great deal, but making too free with the juice of the grape, he fell asleep, and the whole of his riches were taken from him either by our own men or the Spaniards. In the afternoon we recommenced our march in pursuit of the enemy, who had taken the main road to Pampeluna, a strong fortification in their possession: I had not proceeded more than three miles, before I was taken very ill, in consequence, as I thought, of eating a quantity of raw wheat, previous to the commencement of the late battle, and having no drink for nearly three hours after eating it.

I was so very ill that I could not proceed any further, and obtained liberty to leave the ranks. Corporal Phipps was left with me, and I slept in an old house. Next morning, we started for Vittoria, and continued there five days: after this rest, and obtaining my provisions regularly, I soon recovered, and was able to take a view of this city at my leisure. It is a smart-looking town, and contains about six or seven thousand inhabitants: it has a beautiful market-place, and here fresh butter is sold by the pound, as in England.

Neither In Portugal nor on the frontiers of Spain had I ever seen or even heard of such a thing as fresh butter before this period. I saw also nearly all the one hundred and fifty pieces of cannon, and the four hundred and fifteen ammunition waggons, that had been taken near this place, besides several other carriages that were private property. During my stay here, I visited our general hospital, and saw several of the men of our regiment that had been wounded in the late engagement: some of them were in great danger, by reason of the severity of their wounds; but others were hopeful, and expected soon to recover.

On the 29th of June, a party, consisting of men belonging to different regiments, left Vittoria, under the command of Lieutenant Stockford, of our regiment: to this detachment I belonged. During the march, we passed several waggons and carriages that had been thrown over and dashed to pieces by the enemy in their hurry to escape, and in the evening halted in a small village, and the second day took up our quarters in a neat little town. The following day, while the party was marching along, one of the men loaded his musket, and shot at a pig that was grazing by the road side: the officer saw, and would have punished the man; but the pig not being killed, and the man making an ingenious defence, the officer let him off with a severe reprimand.

The prize certainly was a very tempting one, as we were very destitute of food, and had been for the last twelve or fourteen days, with the exception of the days we were in Vittoria; so that we were ready to lay hold of anything that fell in our way, whether living or dead, if eatable; for all along the line of towns, from Vittoria to Pampeluna, the two armies, having passed, had taken or bought nearly all the provisions in the country; indeed at this time it resembled a famine, since we could not obtain anything for money, even if treble its value had been offered.

July 5th; We arrived at a village situated twelve miles from Pampeluna, and there took up our quarters. In the afternoon, a body of Spanish troops came into the town: a man of our detachment and a Spanish soldier quarrelled, and got to fighting: in a few minutes several men on both sides flew to their arms, and there was a running fight across the open fields, before the officer and the greatest part of the men were aware of what had taken place. Lieutenant Stockford immediately ordered the bugle to sound for the men to parade, the rolls were called over, and those men who were absent were soon taken.

One of the offenders was very disorderly and rebellious, but the officer acted promptly; having called out eight men from the ranks, he ordered them to prime and load, declaring, that if the man did not act with more submission, he would shoot him on the spot. Thus, compelled to submit, the next morning he was marched a prisoner to the regiment, which we joined near Pampeluna: he was there given in charge of the rear-guard. About five o'clock in the evening, every man of our party was ordered to fall in, and we underwent a very strict search; first, as to our knapsacks, then our pouches: after these had been done with, every man was ordered to strip: our pockets and the linings of our coats were ransacked, and every guinea, dollar, or shilling, that was found, was taken from us.

The regiment had previously passed the same ordeal, and as much money found as amounted to thirty-two pounds ten shillings and eight pence three farthings each man. A general order had been given for every regiment, which had been amongst the enemy's treasure, to be searched, and the money taken from the men. This was in consequence of the disorderly conduct of some of the soldiers, who were continually so intoxicated, that they could not do their duty.

10th. We marched in the direction of the Pyrenees, and encamped very near them: after which, all the men who had been absent since the Battle of Vittoria underwent a severe scrutiny. Several at the party had their rum stopped for one month: my poor comrade was one of the unhappy number. When the colonel and major came to me, I gave such a good and correct account of myself, that they were both, satisfied that I had been ill; but the man who had rebelled against Lieutenant Stockford was tried by a court-martial, and, as a reward for his conduct, was severely flogged. The next morning our division marched into the Pyrenees, and encamped near a pleasantly situated village, where we halted the next day.

Here cherries and apples were plentiful; and I saw, for the first time in Spain, a number of gooseberry bushes. About the 14th we marched again, and passed through a small town, which had strong walls, with loopholes for musketry instead of cannon: it commanded the beautiful and fertile valley of Bastan, and was very strong and formidable. Here we halted about two hours, and then proceeded on our march, and about two o'clock in the afternoon began to ascend a mountain, which had a very steep ascent for nearly six miles. The day being warm, and the difficulty in ascending great, several of the men were worn out with fatigue, and were obliged to stop behind until evening.

I found it hard work to ascend these lofty hills, for I was then labouring under a complaint to which we were very subject, and had often to leave the ranks. What added to my distress, was the unnecessary strictness of our second major, who refused me liberty to fall out. I at last told him that I really, must have liberty: he then ordered a sergeant, of a tyrannical spirit like himself, to remain with me, who constantly urged me to move forwards, notwithstanding I was so exceedingly ill. We at length overtook the regiment, which was halting on the side of the mountain; but we had only sat about five minutes, when the regiment marched again.

When we had proceeded half a mile, I fell down in the ranks, overpowered with thirst and fatigue. The doctor immediately came to know what was the matter: I told him my complaint, and he ordered me to follow the regiment at my leisure: after a deal of pain and fatigue, I arrived at the camp of our division about ten o'clock at night. Next morning, we moved off again, and got within a short distance of the French Army. About ten o'clock, a tremendous firing commenced between the 2nd Division and the enemy, and at two o'clock the joyful news arrived amongst us that the French were clearly beaten out of Spain.

At this; information, joy and gladness were seen in the countenances of both, officers and men. In the afternoon our division encamped on the summit of one of the loftiest. mountains: just: at this period the heat was so intolerable, that we were very uncomfortable, being almost suffocated. Towards four o'clock a mist came on: it then began to hail and rain, and was so exceedingly cold, that we were nearly frozen. In this condition we spent the night. Nothing could be more hurtful than to march from sixteen to twenty miles in a day, working ourselves into a fever heat, and at night having to lay on the bare ground, frequently in the open air, and often without anything to eat.

This had been the case with myself and thousands of my comrades a great number of times. The next morning, we marched only a short distance, and remained a few days, having working parties mending and widening the roads in the passes. We had also a picquet about two miles in advance. I mounted this picquet, and had an opportunity of visiting some farmhouses, about one mile still further in advance. Nothing could exceed the beautiful appearance of this part of the Pyrenees: from this hill we had a view over a delightful valley full of fruit trees of different sorts, from which we obtained abundance of plums, cherries, and apples.

The mountains in this part of the Pyrenees have a very grand appearance: they are not altogether a chain, but frequently form several independent mountains, rising majestically one above the other for several stages. These mountains extend from the Bay of Biscay to the shores of the Mediterranean Sea, and form the barrier between France and Spain.

About the 16th, the troops had retired to rest at the usual time. At midnight, an express came into our camp, with orders that the roll of each company should be called over. I was astonished at this order, and at first thought the enemy was about to attack us; but I heard nothing more of the matter that night. The next morning the mystery was explained, for we learnt that Lord Aylmer's tent had been robbed of several rich and valuable articles, and he himself put into bodily fear.

As soon as the thieves were gone, the order for calling over the rolls was sent to the whole of our division; but no man of our regiment or brigade was missing. Two men, however, of the second brigade, belonging to the 24th Regiment, were absent. Lord Aylmer commanded this brigade, and had a guard over his tent: it was supplied by the regiments in turn, but he allowed the sentinel, instead of watching, to lie down and sleep; and he was thus rewarded by the very men whom he had befriended; for the two men of the above regiment, who had often mounted this guard, proved to be the thieves, part of the property being found upon their persons. The general told them that they might prepare for death, for nothing could save them.

On the 18th we moved up to the front, and were posted near the French Army. This day I bought a fat sheep of a Spaniard, which cost six shillings and two pence, and weighed about twenty-five pounds.

On the 19th I mounted the advanced guard, and in the evening each man had to fetch a load of sticks for the fire. At dusk, I and another went for our quantum of wood, and coming to a hovel, found a sheep, which had taken shelter there. We immediately brought home our load, and acquainted the corporal with what we had seen, promising, if he would allow us to go and kill it, to let him have a quarter of it. He consented, and we repaired to the spot: I then took my knife, and killed the poor animal. To whom the sheep belonged, I know not, but probably to the French, as it was between the two armies, and on the French side of the Pyrenees: but to us it made little matter who was the owner, we were hungry, and glad of such an opportunity of satisfying our craving appetites.

On the 23rd I mounted this guard the second time, the men whom we relieved had killed a young bullock on the previous night. This day I went so far in advance, that I came within a very short distance, of a French village, but dared not to enter, lest I should be taken prisoner, as it was almost certain, that the French Army had possession of it. I turned back, and entering a valley, arrived at a small farmhouse: the first thing I asked for was bread; the farmer said he had none, but gave me some apples, and a quantity of salt, which was very acceptable indeed.

This night, our most advanced sentinel was found asleep on his post: had the enemy advanced, they would most probably have surprised the army, and taken many prisoners. The man was punished for his neglect of duty; though not so severely as he otherwise would have been, had it been under different circumstances; that is, had there been more danger.

In the afternoon of the 25th orders came for every man, not on duty, to repair to the camp of the second brigade, to witness the execution of the two men who had robbed Lord Aylmer's tent. The next morning, by daylight, we fell in, and passed on our march about twenty thousand Spaniards, lying in encampment. We arrived at the camp of the 24th Regiment, which was nearly six miles north of ours, and saw the two poor wretched culprits at their prayers, surrounded by the whole of the women of that regiment, who were bitterly lamenting the sad condition of the unhappy men.

The prisoners were dressed in white, and were preparing for death in the midst of their kind-hearted country-women. Our regiment came to the place of execution, and formed with several other regiments into a large square, and there saw the awful preparations going forward. The provost marshal had pitched upon a tree which had a large arm, something like a gallows: he had also prepared two ladders, one on each side of the tree, having a plank from one ladder to the other, thereby forming a kind of drop. He had a number of men to assist him; and ropes were fixed to the foot of each ladder, so that the moment the signal should be given, the men, by pulling the ropes, were to liberate the plank, and thus let the men drop.

While these things were going on, a large body of French infantry, that were posted on the opposite hills, got under arms, expecting, no doubt, that we were going to attack them: we could see them moving about as distinctly as possible. At length the prisoners were brought into the square by the provost marshal's guard; the proceedings of the court martial were then read; all were unmoved, until the sentence, that they were to be hanged, was pronounced. At this period there was a visible change in the countenance of every man, for we all felt for these unfortunate wretches, who were doomed to suffer a shameful death in the sight of both armies.

They were now ordered forward to the gallows, and assisted on to the plank, and the ropes were adjusted: they confessed their guilt, and hoped that their fate would be a warning to the soldiers not to be guilty of the like crime: the signal was then given, and the unhappy men were launched into eternity. After the execution, we marched to our respective encampments, and there learnt that the enemy had already begun those offensive operations, which brought on the bloody contests of the Pyrenees.

Lieutenant-General Sir Rowland Hill

CHAPTER 16

Soult is Sent Against Lord Wellington

Lord Wellington, after the brilliant successes which he had gained over the enemy, had pursued the fugitive army without loss of time to the frontiers of France, and had established the Allied Army in the passes of the western Pyrenees. General Byng's brigade, and a Spanish corps, lay at the pass of Roncesvalles: Sir Lowry Cole; with his division, was at Viscarret, to support these troops: General Picton's division was stationed at Olaque, in reserve. The, valley of Bastan was occupied by Sir Rowland Hill's division, and the Conde Amaranthe's Spanish corps.

Our division was posted with the light division on the heights of Santa Barbara, at the town of Vera, and in the Puerto d'Echalar. The 6th Division was in reserve at Estevan. Sir Thomas Graham undertook the siege of St. Sebastian, and the Conde del Abisbal, with a body of Spaniards, the blockade of Pampeluna.

Buonaparte, who was at this time occupied in Germany, being alarmed at the progress of our army, determined to make an effort to retrieve his Spanish affairs, and pluck from us the laurels we had won: for this purpose, he appointed Marshal Soult, unquestionably the best general in the French service, *Lieutenant l'Empereur*, and commander in chief of all his forces in Spain and the south of France. Armed with this comprehensive authority, he arrived at the scene of action on the 13th of July, bringing with him large reinforcements.

On the 25th, Marshal Soult attacked, with a body of nearly forty thousand men, General Byng's post at Roncesvalles, and forcing the pass, compelled him to retreat, which he did in good order, to Zubiri. In the afternoon of the same day, an immense body of the enemy assailed General Hill's position, at the Puerto de Maya, at the head of the valley of Bastan, and forced him to give way. At this critical juncture, Major-General Barnes' brigade of our division hastened to his support, and enabled him to regain his posts: however, in consequence of the retreat of General Byng, he afterwards, withdrew to Irurita. The troops employed on this occasion, during an engagement of seven hours, fought with desperation, and every regiment charged with the bayonet. The conduct of the 82nd Regiment, of our division, was much admired.

We received intelligence of these transactions as we were returning from witnessing the execution of the two men who robbed Lord Aylmer's tent: and, on our approach to the contested spot, found, to our great regret, that we could render our brave fellows no assistance whatever, though we had a full view of them, by reason of a tremendous ravine, which it was impossible to pass: besides, we expected soon to have plenty of employment on our own account. We escaped for this time, and after having been under arms a considerable period, we ascended to the top of a mountain: thence, on the morning of the 26th, we retreated to Pampeluna.

On the 27th, the enemy arrived in front of our positions near Pampeluna, and fell with tremendous fury upon the third and fourth Divisions, under Generals Picton and Cole, while they were in the act of taking up their ground, and a sanguinary conflict ensued. Several of the regiments had to charge with the bayonet four or five times: the enemy at length gave way, and were driven back with immense loss.

Finding himself thus foiled, Soult now directed his efforts against General Hill, who was marching upon Lizasso, followed by a large body of the enemy. He afterwards strongly reinforced this body, and proceeded to adopt measures for attacking Sir Rowland Hill's division, taking at the same time possession of a prodigious mountain in advance of our division stationed at Marcalain. Lord Wellington, anticipating his design, determined to be before hand with him, and draw off his attention from General Hill, by reducing him to the necessity of attending to the defence of his own position: for this purpose, he immediately gave orders for General Picton to turn the enemy's left by the road to Roncesvalles, and for our division, under the Earl of Dalhousie, to assail the mountain in our front.

Accordingly, on the 29th, we set out upon this enterprise. In the afternoon I was ordered on a reconnoitring party, consisting of a corporal and six privates, under the command of Captain Gledstanes, and a lieutenant. We moved in the direction of the enemy, and posted ourselves within two hundred yards of their sentinels: three of us were placed on sentry, having strict orders to fire the moment we saw a

French soldier move towards us. The captain, lieutenant, and one of the men, ascended one of the most lofty mountains, to survey the French position; after which they returned, and the sentinels were called in.

A farmhouse being near, we called and obtained refreshment, and then joined the regiment, which had received orders to advance at one o'clock in the morning: at the appointed time we fell in, without the sound of the bugle, and moved off, passing over the same grounds and came to the house where we had been refreshed the day before. We passed the house, and advanced towards the enemy, who were posted at a distance of not more than eight hundred yards from it.

As our regiment was ascending the mountain, we received a volley from their advanced guard: they then opened such a terrible fire upon us, that we were obliged to measure our steps back in quick time to the farmhouse. There being a wall in a line with the house, several men were posted behind it; others went into the house, and fired out of the windows and doorway.

Having good cover, we opened a most deliberate and destructive fire upon our enemies, and although greatly superior to us in numbers, we kept them in check, having firm possession of the farmhouse and garden, from which they could not dislodge us. They at length retired to the top of their own position, and we received orders to leave the house instantly, and to move round the hill, and attack them at another point: but we had not got more than half a mile, before our company was sent back to keep possession of the house and garden, and to place sentinels to watch the enemy in another direction. Having returned and taken possession of the house, I and my comrade were placed on sentry together on a footpath, which led up from the main body of the enemy: our situation was so conspicuous, that we could see the movements of both armies.

When our brigade had got round the hill, they immediately advanced to the summit; and notwithstanding the enemy's fire, carried it at the point of the bayonet. No troops could have acted better than this part of our division. They then advanced to the next hill, and dislodged the enemy with the same deadly instrument. Nothing could withstand the gallantry of our brigade; they bore down all before them. About two miles below the path over which I was stationed, a division of French infantry, and several regiments of cavalry, had taken shelter behind a hill; but a brisk fire of cannon and musketry having been opened upon them, the cavalry began to retreat one by one:

when they came to the place where the danger was greatest, they rode full gallop. Several of them were killed, the rest narrowly escaped; their infantry having to stand to cover their retreat.

At this period our troops moved forward with redoubled vigour: the enemy gave way in all directions, and abandoned the position they had been so anxious to obtain. When the engagement was over, out regiment collected at the house before mentioned: we then as on other occasions of the kind, began to enquire who was killed and who was wounded: the first person mentioned was our second major; he had received a ball in his neck, or rather in his windpipe, which killed him instantly.

As soon as this was generally known amongst us, joy was seen in every countenance, and I verily thought we should have had three cheers, for several of the men began to cry "hip! hip!" which was always the signal for cheering. He was a cruel man to us, and his death was considered as a happy release. Our total loss this morning was about thirty-one killed and wounded, and we had one man taken prisoner: he had been placed on sentry before daylight, and not being relieved at our first retreat, fell into the hands of the enemy.

While these operations were going on. Lord Wellington sent troops to the support of General Hill. The enemy appeared before his position late in the morning; but he gave them such a warm reception, that they were glad to seek safety by flight, especially as Lord Wellington had proceeded in person to intercept them. On the next day they took up a strong position, with two divisions to cover their rear, in the pass of Donna Maria. This pass Sir Rowland Hill and Lord Dalhousie were ordered to force. Accordingly, on the 31st, our division set out on this service, and in the afternoon halted within four miles of the pass. Having learnt that the enemy were cooking, Lord Dalhousie gave orders for the division to be put in motion, intending to take them by surprise. We no sooner approached the pass, than our brigade filed off to attack a strong body of the enemy, which was posted on a hill that projected from the pass, the 2nd and 3rd Brigades moving forward.

The mountains being rough, and covered with trees, were difficult to ascend; but we soon surmounted these difficulties, and coming up with the enemy, immediately went to work: they were determined to defend this post to the last extremity, and a most destructive firing commenced, the balls cutting down the branches above our heads. A ball struck a poor fellow near me on the shinbone, which was broken in pieces: his cries were truly lamentable. We still advanced to the pass,

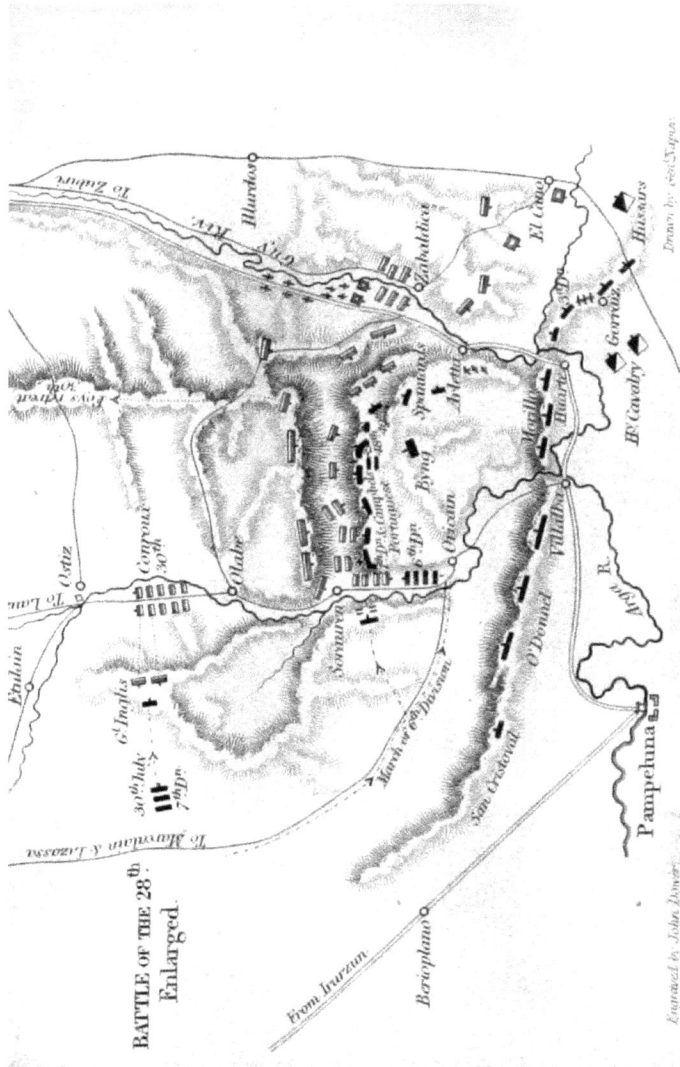

BATTLE of THE 28th.
Enlarged.

Pampeluna

From Irurzun

Bexoplano

To Marcalaw y Larossa

San Cristoval

O'Donnel

Villalba

Huarte

Zabaldica

El Cano

Husars

Br Cavalry

Goroiz

Magdl

Ardanz

Byng

Spaniards

Portuguese

Lizazo

Olabe

Convent 30th

To Lanz

Villaba

To Zubiri

Huarlos

ARGA Riv.

Foys Ridge Top

Ostiz

Enlain

6th Inglis

30th July

7th Dgns

Oricain

March or Explosion

Ramasay

Drawn by Col Napier

Engraved by John Dower

but the enemy pushing forward in vast masses, forced us to give way a little: we, however, soon rallied and after a deal of hard fighting gained the summit of the mountain, at the point of the bayonet.

A very serious mistake took place during our ascent. While Sir Rowland Hill's corps were ascending on the other side of the pass, hearing the reports of our muskets, and our balls passing over them, they thought we were the enemy, and fired upon us: we also fired on them in return, and several lives were lost. This error being rectified, we carried the pass, notwithstanding the vigorous resistance of the enemy, and remained masters of the heights. After this we descended into the valley and encamped, the enemy having scampered off. There was not one man of our company left, except myself, to pitch the tent, or to draw the provisions. The loss of our regiment was very great, having about thirty killed and wounded; but what made the thing most affecting was, that the greatest number of the men killed, and wounded were married, and had families at home.

The next morning, our division moved off in pursuit of the enemy, and encamped near Vera, the fortified town I have, mentioned before. On the 2nd of August we ascended the most lofty part of the Pyrenees, and found that the enemy had lost on the 1st of August about a thousand mules loaded with bread, intended for the relief of Pampeluna; besides being obliged to throw a great deal of their baggage into a river.

Towards evening we came up with two divisions of the enemy near the Puerto d'Echalar, the last post they held in Spain, and without waiting for us, our second brigade, under General Barnes, commenced a most vigorous attack upon them. our brigade followed close after to assist, but our aid was not required; the gallantry of General Barnes, with his brigade, completely drove the enemy from their position into France. Thus, we cleared this part of Spain, for the second time, of its worst enemy; the army of Joseph Buonaparte; and in the evening our division encamped near the town of Echalar.

3rd. Our division ascended to the top of the mountains, and encamped within a mile of our old ground, after an absence of nine days, one part or other of the army having been engaged with the enemy eight days out of that period.

The total loss sustained by the English, &c,, from the 25th of July to the 28th, was nearly four thousand three hundred in killed, wounded, and taken; and that of the enemy amounted to nearly fifteen thousand. The particulars of the losses sustained by the Allies are as follows: two majors, nine captains, twelve lieutenants, five ensigns, three staff, and five hundred and twenty-seven non-commissioned officers and privates, killed; one general staff, twelve lieutenant-colonels, thirteen majors, forty-four captains, eighty-one lieutenants, thirty-six ensigns, six staff, with three thousand one hundred and seventy-four non-commissioned officers and private, and five horses, wounded; five captains, four lieutenants, four ensigns, one staff, four hundred and forty non-commissioned officers and privates, and one horse, missing. The Spanish loss was twenty-six men killed, twelve officers and one hundred and fifty-five men wounded, and eleven men missing.

On the 30th, the British loss was eighty-one killed, and four hundred and sixty-nine wounded. The Portuguese loss was very great. I have not the number of killed and wounded from the 31st July to the 2nd August: the grand total of the Allies must have been nearly six thousand in killed, wounded, and missing; for in no part of the Peninsular War did we suffer more than during the severe contests across the lofty Pyrenees. We lay in our camp very tranquil until the 14th; it was then reported, that the 15th being Napoleon's birthday, the French Army intended to make another attempt to force the different passes of the Pyrenees, in order to raise the siege of St. Sebastian, and compel the English Army to retreat in the direction of Vittoria.

We certainly expected some attempts would be made for that purpose; consequently, on the 15th, our knapsacks were ready packed, and our arms piled, no man being allowed to leave the camp for more than ten minutes. In this situation we waited the attack of the enemy; but notwithstanding the zeal of the French Army, and their love for Buonaparte, no movements were made towards us. They probably remembered their late defeats and losses; for instead of driving us back into the heart of Spain, as they had fully anticipated, they had everywhere met with discomfiture and disgrace, and had retired into their own country in dismay and confusion,

About the 17th we were again in very great distress for want of food, having been nearly three days without receiving either bread or biscuit: there were a few loaves of bread brought into our camp by Spanish peasants, which were sold at two shillings and sixpence the pound; and even at this enormous price they were bought up with eagerness; if there had been ten times the quantity they would have met with a ready sale. During these three days' famine, we had perhaps twenty reports that the commissary had received a supply of bread;

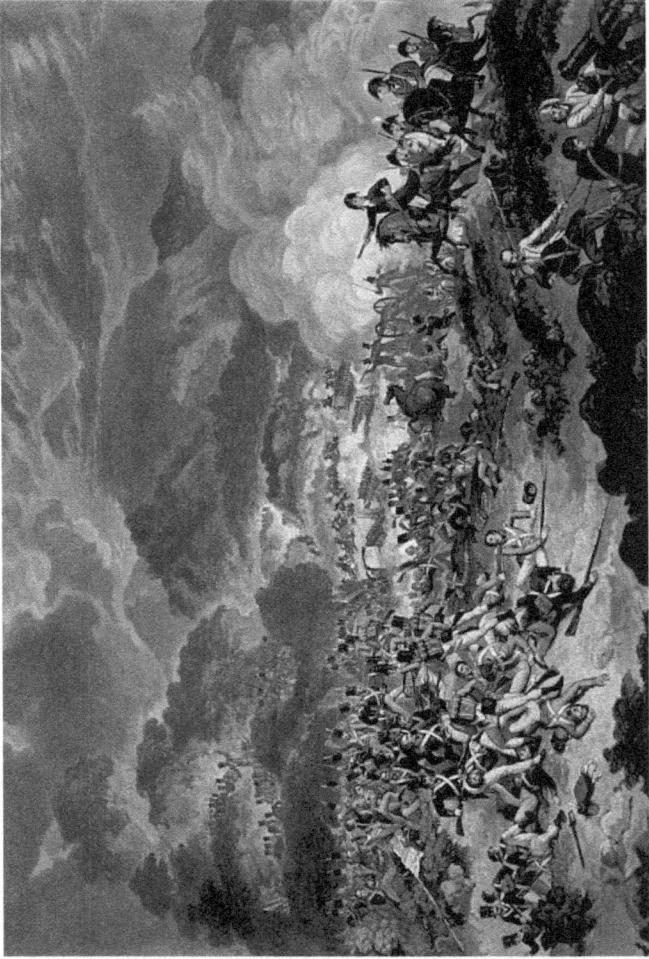

BATTLE OF THE PYRENEES

but we were as often mortified to learn that they were false. On the evening of the 3rd day our supplies came up, and every man received his proper allowance. During this privation, however, we received our beef and rum regularly, so that our wants were not so great as they had been on other occasions, when we were without provision, of every description for two or three days together:

About the 21st I mounted the bullock guard: the next morning I had to ascend one of the mountains for five of the best bullocks to be killed for that day's allowance. On arriving at the summit, I found myself actually above the clouds: the sky was clear and serene, but below it was cloudy, and in some parts of the valleys both misty and rainy. I descended with the bullocks through the mists and clouds into the valley where the division was encamped.

On the 29th, I mounted the guard a second time since our return from Pampeluna. Being, Sunday, we had divine service performed by a minister of the church of England. I stole from the guard, got into the rear of one of the regiments, and heard the prayers read: after which a short sermon was preached. This was the only sermon I had ever heard since May 1811, it being two years and three months. I was delighted with the clergyman, and paid the greatest attention to his profitable discourse. After the sermon was ended, I returned to my guard, but it was not known that I had been absent. In the afternoon I was sent to the top of the mountain, with orders to the herdsmen of our commissary.

Being a clear day, I could discern objects at the distance of fifty miles or more. Bayonne appeared to be very near. I could perceive hundreds of towns and villages. In that part of France next the Pyrenees, most of the houses are white, so that they can be seen distinctly at a great distance. Nothing could exceed the beautiful appearance of the country below me.

On Monday the 30th, I was relieved, joined my company, cooked my dinner as usual, everything appearing tranquil: but about two o'clock an express arrived from Lord Wellington, ordering the 51st, 68th, 82nd, and Chasseurs Britanniques, to move off immediately in the direction of St. Sebastian. We certainly expected that our brigade was going to assist in the storming of that very strong fortification. The bugles speedily sounded, down came the tents, which were packed up, and in less than forty minutes we were on our way.

Previous to our march, orders had been given to some of the divisions to furnish twenty men each regiment, to join the storming party at St. Sebastian. We passed the tree on which the two men of the 24th Regiment were hanged; we also passed the light division, and a division of Spaniards, and encamped within three miles of Lord Wellington's headquarters. Here we received a draft from England, consisting of sixteen men, and the 82nd, one of about one hundred and fifty.

Early on the morning of the 31st of August we were under arms, and about seven o'clock marched through headquarters, and began to ascend one of the mountains: but before we gained the summit, the sound of musketry was distinctly heard. Arriving at the top of the hill, we saw a regiment of Portuguese infantry retiring before the enemy, who had crossed the river by the fords, the bridges having been destroyed. They were on the opposite hill, to the number, as nearly as could be ascertained, of twenty-three thousand men; besides, several pieces of cannon, known by the name of mule-guns, from being carried by the mules, the carriage on one side and the gun on the other.

We had no sooner formed, than the enemy opened a fire open us from these guns, which on this occasion did little or no execution. The French wanted to raise the siege of St. Sebastian, and were determined, by an overwhelming force, to gain their object. We had only four British regiments, and one regiment of Portuguese, which had already given way, to oppose this mighty army.

Our regiment was now ordered forward, and extended all along the front of the brigade We loaded our pieces, and waited for the enemy, who were advancing, having taken our stand about four hundred yards from the summit of the hill, directly in front of the 82nd Regiment. When they came within two hundred yards, we began to fire upon them, every man being directed, to take deliberate aim. The enemy having approached within one hundred yards of us, we retreated deliberately, keeping up a most destructive fire. When we nearly reached the summit of the mountain, we formed, and waited till they arrived within twenty yards. We then fired a volley, gave three cheers, and rushed upon them with fixed bayonets. This caused them to give way, and we pursued them exultingly to the bottom of the hill, calling them in the Spanish language, "*Malditos ladrones!*" and other opprobrious names.

One of our men, who it was said, had wounded himself at the Battle of Vittoria, ran in front of most of the skirmishers to redeem his character: I followed him until he received a ball in his belly: he then turned round, and made what haste he could to the top of the hill, crying and groaning in the bitterest manner. He afterwards recovered, and was able to do his duty. The enemy having obtained a strong reinforcement, now advanced in close column, their drums beating in order to keep them together. We again retreated, and I narrowly escaped being taken prisoner; for I was almost exhausted with running. As we retreated, we kept up a steady and well-directed fire, and gained the summit of the hill in good order, not having a single man taken prisoner.

It was now thought prudent to retire before this column to the next range of hills. We kept up a constant fire as we retired, and took up a position on a hill; at the extremity of which I and about twenty more were stationed: there being several trees, each man posted himself behind one, and began to discharge his piece. With firing so often, my flint became worn out, and I retired about fifteen yards to the rear, and fixed a new one into my musket. While thus employed, Lieutenant Skene told me that George Noble and two others of our company were wounded: I said, I was sorry for it, and immediately resumed my place; but had only fired one shot, when a ball struck me, entering my left side, a little below my heart.

At first, I felt nothing; in about ten seconds, however, I fell to the ground, turned sick and faint, and expected every moment to expire, having an intolerable burning pain in my left side. I thought it was all over with me, being confident that I had received a mortal wound. I lay on the ground about five minutes, when the sergeant-major, who was near the spot; ordered two of the men to take me to the rear. They attempted to lift me up; but I begged of them to let me alone, saying, "For God's, sake, let me die in peace!" the men then let me drop on the ground again, no doubt thinking I was actually dying.

The sergeant-major seeing what they had done, said, in a loud tone, "Take him away to the rear, for he is not dead." They then raised me up, loosed the straps of my knapsacks, and took off my belts: I opened my coat and waistcoat, and putting my hand, against my side, found a lump occasioned by the ball nearly as large as a hen's egg. My shirt and trowsers were drenched with blood. In this condition I started to the rear, assisted by the men above mentioned: I had not proceeded more than fifty yards, before I was deserted by them. The shots from the enemy, at this period flew so exceedingly fast, that the men were afraid of being killed, so that I was left to take care of myself, but Captain Gledstanes being near the spot, I said, "Sir, am I to be left in this condition, to be killed or taken by, the enemy?"

"No, my man," said this amiable officer, "I will assist you;" and immediately seizing hold of my right arm, and giving me a stick, in my left hand, conducted me out of the reach of the enemy's balls. He then gave me in charge of two soldiers, who assisted me to the place where the regiment had collected, and where the surgeons were in attendance to dress the wounds, and to render that assistance which is required on occasions of this kind. I never think of Captain Gledstanes but with pleasure: I was indebted to him for my life; for had he not thus kindly assisted me, I should in all probability have been either killed or taken by the enemy, who were not more than two hundred yards from me.

I often wonder I was not wounded a second time. As I lay gasping upon the ground, several of my comrades, (Irishmen,) came to me, saying, "Arrah! Green, my poor fellow, are you much hurt?" and consoled me as well as they could: some gave me water and others rum to drink, and thus testified their respect and kindness towards me. At length a surgeon began to examine me: he took off my shirt, and ran his probe into the wound. In the meantime, the Colonel of the Chasseurs Britanniques was brought to this spot, wounded in the head; and the surgeon left me in my naked state to attend on him. In a few seconds, however, Mr. Reid, our Regimental Surgeon, came to me, and ran his little finger into my side, to clear it of any substance that might be lodged in the wound. I cried aloud by reason of the pain it occasioned.

"Silence!" said the surgeon, "it is for your good." The ball could not be extracted. A little dry lint was put over the wound, and a bandage bound tight round my body: my clothes were put on, and I was laid on the ground, but was so full of pain, that I could not rest more than two minutes in any one posture. In a short time, several of the officers collected on the spot where I lay. Captain Gledstanes gave me an excellent character to the colonel, saying, no man of our regiment had behaved better, or shown more courage than I had done while charging the enemy down the mountain. Colonel Hawkins, who had been my captain for five years, said, he was sorry to see me in my present situation; but if I recovered, he would remember my soldier-like conduct, and do something for me. I now made my will, which was as follows: "If I die in consequence of my wound, I wish for my arrears, clothing money, and prize money, to be given to my comrade James Mann, who has always been my faithful friend."

Captain Gledstanes said he would see that my wish was complied with, if James outlived me. Having lost my musket, knapsack, and accoutrements (for one of our men had taken them to the rear,) and not being able to look after them myself, I begged of the colonel to allow James to go with me into the rear for a day or two, that he might assist me in recovering them. The colonel very kindly granted my request, and allowed my comrade to accompany me.

After settling these things, I and several other wounded men were provided with mules to carry us: we immediately proceeded to the rear, but had only got three or four miles when a dreadful storm came on; the rain fell in torrents, the flashes of lightning were most alarming, and the claps of thunder loud, and quickly succeeding each other. The pack-saddle on which I rode was covered with an oil-cloth; the water ran from the saddle-cloth, down my trowsers, into my shoes, and out of them, as though they had been springs or fountains, and in a short time I was almost drowned. I wished to lie down, and every hovel we came to I begged to be put into it, that I might rest.

Being in a miserable plight; drenched with blood, sweat, and rain; fatigued, full of pain, and never expecting to see the hospital, I thought every moment would be my last: when I requested James to put me into a shepherd's hut, he smiled, and consoled me by saying, "You shall not die yet."

After nearly three hours' ride, we arrived at a small village. I was then taken off the mule, and assisted into the house: my clothes were taken off, and I was put to bed: the woman of the house, when she saw them strip me, exclaimed with emotion, "Jesu! Maria! Jesu! Maria!" and prayed for me. The sympathy of the old woman affected me very much, and brought to my mind my dear and aged relatives at home. I thought, if this poor woman, to whom I was a stranger, could be so moved with a sight of my condition, what would their feelings have been had they known it. The night passed over slowly, the bed was very hard, and so over-run with fleas, that I could not sleep. I wished for the morning, and when it came, I was still restless and full of pain, both in body and mind.

The baggage of our brigade was encamped near this village: the captain of my company commanded it. We sent my comrade to make our cases known to him, and he very kindly sent a guinea to be divided amongst us. With this supply of money we bought some provisions from the inhabitants, who willingly let us have such as they had, giving us into the bargain whatever cider we wished to drink.

In the afternoon, an old soldier, who had been used to the hospitals, came round and dressed our wounds: the old man did very well, for after he had dressed my wound I seemed, easier. We sent a man to headquarters, to draw provisions, and procure medical assistance: he returned on the 3rd September with our bread and meat, but had drunk and sold the rum: had he been with the regiment, he would have paid dear for his base conduct.

A surgeon arrived with thirty mules to carry us to the general hospital: he dressed our wounds, and then gave orders for us to march at two o'clock in the afternoon. This being the fourth day, since we had been wounded, our wounds were very sore: some were crying by reason of excessive pain in their fractured limbs. As for myself, I wept like a child. We were the worst off in descending the mountains: the mules slided down for three or four yards together; and how I got to the end of my journey I can scarcely tell: Sergeant Currie fell from his mule, and narrowly escaped falling down a steep precipice. We at length arrived at Lord Wellington's headquarters, and were put into the town hall, where we had to lie on the bare stones.

On the 4th we marched again, and passed over the ground on which we had been engaged. I saw the tree where I received my wound, and after riding over the field of the late battle, we began to descend the mountains. Our sufferings while descending these lofty hills were indescribable: I really never expected to reach the bottom alive, it was like cutting my body to pieces. I cried, screamed, prayed, and wished to die: my companions were in the same way; some were praying, others weeping and moaning, and we presented a scene of the completest misery and wretchedness. We at length arrived at the bottom of the mountains, and were quartered at General Graham's headquarters, where we had again to lie on the bare floor without a covering.

Here we heard of the fall of St. Sebastian: it was taken by storm on the 31st of August, the very day on which I was wounded, after a severe conflict. The enemy made a desperate attempt to raise the siege, in which they failed; our gallant band, soon after I was wounded, routed them, drove them back again across the Bidassoa with great loss, and forced them to leave St. Sebastian to its fate. The loss of our regiment on that day, in covering the siege, was ninety killed and wounded, besides officers. The total loss sustained by our army in the conflict at St. Sebastian, from July 28th to August 31st, including the assault, taking the Portuguese into the account, is as follows: one lieutenant-colonel, two majors, eight captains, twenty lieutenants, ten ensigns, three staff, and seven hundred and sixteen non-commissioned officers and privates, killed; three general officers, three lieutenant-colonels, two majors, twenty-five captains, forty-eight lieutenants, twenty-four ensigns, and one thousand five hundred and ninety-two non-commissioned officers and privates, wounded; one lieutenant and forty-four privates, missing.—The next day we reached Passages about noon, and were safely lodged in the general hospital.

CHAPTER 17

Arrives at Plymouth

After remaining a short time in the hospital, I was put into a ward, consisting of fifteen wounded men belonging to different regiments: nothing could exceed the miserable appearance of the patients, for some of us were almost lost with vermin, not having been able to clean ourselves for several days. Every man had a kind of bed made of two biscuit-bags sewed together, and filled with fern, or what we call brackens, which was very comfortable in comparison with what we had been accustomed to.

On the 8th of September the hospital stores arrived from England, and we were served out with everything that could conduce to our comfort and health. Each man was provided with a harden bed-tick filled with straw, two blankets, one pair of sheets, and one rug: this happy change caused us partly to forget our late misfortunes. I also found my knapsack and necessaries, which went on board a vessel opposite the hospital door.

Passages is very properly so named, for a river or arm of the sea runs through the town, leaving only a very narrow road: the yard-arms of the vessels nearly touch the windows of the houses. St. Sebastian is only two miles from this place. We were annoyed with the noise of the guns from the castle, but it surrendered the 8th of September, holding out only eight days longer than the town. The surgeons attended twice a day to dress the wounds of their patients, and every medical officer was attentive to his charge, and did all that could be done for our recovery. One morning after the surgeon had dressed my wound, he clapped me on the back, telling me I should soon be able to have another shot at the French.

Among the fifteen wounded men in our ward, there were three that had received wounds in the body, besides myself; ten that were wounded either in their legs or arms; and one that had a fracture occasioned by a fall. One of them, a man of our regiment, belonging to Captain Gough's company, had received a ball through his breastbone: whenever the surgeon took off the dressing, the blood and water gushed out of the wound as if it had been pumped out with considerable force: this was the case every time he was dressed. The poor fellow endured his misery with the greatest patience and resignation, and died about the 16th of the month.

Another, belonging to Captain Gledstane's company, had received a wound in his left arm, so near the shoulder that it could not be amputated. His condition was indeed deplorable; for, in addition to his being wounded on the 31st of August, he was taken by the French, who stripped him naked, and left him exposed in that condition during the night. He was found on the 2nd of September, and conducted to this hospital. When the surgeons examined him, they found that the flies had not only struck his wound, but other parts of his body; and his arm presented a most horrid spectacle: it was literally alive. The surgeons did all in their power to save the poor man, but in vain. His agony was beyond description. He died about the 17th of the month, and was not more than twenty-four years of age.

A third, who belonged the guards, lay in the next bed to mine: he had received a severe wound in his shinbone, which seemed to be doing well; and we were often reckoning of enjoying ourselves at Chelsea: but, how vain was his hope! His wound turned so bad, that he was obliged to undergo amputation. Three days after, one of the arteries getting loose, the surgeon was sent for: his thigh was opened to take up the artery, but the surgeon could not get the thigh bone covered again; it was more than an inch longer than it ought to have been. The consequence was, that the man had to undergo a second operation: he was very cheerful during the painful process, but died the same night.

A fourth, who belonged to the same regiment, had received a ball through his right breast: it passed out at his shoulder-blade. When he drew his breath, the dressing seemed as though it would have gone into his body. He lingered a few days, and then died, apparently without pain. Although he lay in the bed next to mine, he had been removed to the deadhouse some hours before I knew that he was gone.

The fifth case is that of a man of Captain Gough's company, whose name was Church: he had received a ball through his groin, but was in a very hopeful way. Church was very ill-natured with some of the wounded men, because they moaned and disturbed him. He said, if he had lost both his legs, he could do without making so much noise.

However, on the 18th, he was taken worse, and began to moan himself most bitterly: on the 21st he died, having been delirious two whole days.

The mortality in our ward was very great: of four men who had received body wounds, three were already dead; and I remained only in a precarious state, for the ball could not be extracted. The medical men gave me no encouragement, nor held out any hopes of my recovery. All was horror: five or six, out of fifteen, were already dead, and several of the others were in great danger: the deadhouse was never entirely clear of corpses from the different parts of the hospital.

On the 20th of September an order came for all the men, that could be removed, to be embarked on board of transports, and sent to St. Andero with as little delay as possible. The general doctor came round to select those whom he thought proper: he appointed me as one that was to be removed. I objected going to sea, urging that sea-sickness would distress me, and put me to much pain: the doctor would not listen to my reasoning, but gave orders for my removal to St. Andero.

About the 24th we were embarked on board a ship fitted up for the reception of the wounded men. Every man having a bed to himself, I was placed in that part of the vessel where the motion is felt least, and had every attention paid me during the voyage. The captain of the vessel and the ship's crew were very kind unto us. Our voyage was pleasant and comfortable: we passed along the Bay of Biscay, the swell of which was great, and the ship rolled very much, but I was, in a very singular manner, free from seasickness, which I so much dreaded.

About the 2nd of October we landed at St. Andero, but I was so exceedingly ill and lame that I walked almost double. One of our men carried my knapsack, and I followed like a poor distressed and aged man, bending beneath a load of years. Although the hospital to which we were going was not far distant I found it one of the hardest tasks I had ever met with to get thither.

At length I arrived at the convent called St. Antonia, which is a large and spacious building, well calculated for the reception of wounded men. As soon as we had got into the hospital the men were sent into different apartments, or wards, and every one of us was provided with a bed and bedding. All our regimental clothing was taken from us, and put into the storeroom: each man received a complete suit of hospital clothing, consisting, of a long coat, a flannel waistcoat, a pair of trowsers, and a shirt, to which was added a flannel cap. Our uniform was complete, all being dressed in white.

I had not been here more than three days, when I was again taken very ill, and expected to die. I could not rest for whole nights together: the doctors frequently gave me laudanum: and three doses have been given during one evening, with little or no effect. My life was a burden to me; often have I been constrained to weep over my calamitous situation, I continued until Christmas before my complaint took a turn: one thing, however, transpired that in some measure alleviated my afflictions; that is, on the 20th of October I was invalided for England. The thoughts of once more seeing my native country caused me to bear my pain and troubles with resignation.

About the 16th of November, one of the wounded soldiers was brought to the surgery to undergo amputation: the operation had already begun, when I was seized, with the cramp in my wounded side. I made five times more noise than the poor man who was losing his limb; and there is no doubt but my pain, while it lasted; was greater than his.

During the winter, the yellow fever got amongst the soldiers in the different hospitals: many men were carried off by this fatal disease. Only a few however in our hospital were attacked. The moment a case of this sort was discovered, the person was removed without delay to a hospital appropriated to cases of yellow fever alone.

One afternoon, a man of our regiment called me by the name of my county: in a few minutes after a soldier, who laid opposite to me, came to enquire what part of Lincolnshire I came from. I said, from Louth. The man answered with a sort of delight, "Why, I come from Tetney." By this incident we became acquainted. His name is Christopher Ludlam: he belonged to the 59th Regiment, and had received a wound on the 31st of August, at the storming of St. Sebastian. His wound was in a bad state through ill treatment, and the consequence was, he had to undergo amputation of the arm near the shoulder. Ludlam was a religious man, and he often lamented to me his want of zeal and Christian courage.

He soon recovered, was sent to Chelsea to pass the board of general officers, and obtained a pension of one shilling per day: he now resides at Kelstern, near Louth. In consequence of a delay of my accounts from the regiment, I was detained a considerable period. I have mentioned before that I found a Bible amongst the ruin and desolation of the Battle of Vittoria: often, whilst in this dreary place, did I peruse the pages of that blessed book. Although I knew but little about religion, yet I felt a degree of comfort from this delightful exercise.

At one time I was led to adopt the language of Jacob, that, "if the Lord would indeed bring me back to my kindred and people, I would devote the residue of my life to his service." This resolution I frequently repeated, with prayers and tears; and from this time, I began, to recover, although but slowly. I walked a little every day with the assistance of two crutches, but was obliged to take very short steps, for if I stepped too far, it brought the cramp in my wounded side. In about ten or twelve days my crutches were laid aside, and two sticks substituted in their place. In the month of December, I was sent to the recovery ward, but remained very weak. In this ward was a man belonging to the 59th Regiment, called Farral, who had the misfortune to lose both his eyes at the storming of St. Sebastian: this poor fellow could walk about the hospital without a guide; and in order to try him, we often laid things in his way; but he was never known to stumble, or walk over them; and although he was doomed to perpetual darkness, he was very cheerful, and apparently, comfortable and happy in his sad condition.

In January 1814, I left St. Antonia hospital, and joined the depot, which was then in some wooden houses about half a mile to the west of the hospital. These houses had been made and put together in England: each part was numbered, so that we had only to put them together, and set them up. They were very imperfect: the wind on some occasions unroofed a part, and left us exposed to the rain: in fine weather they were delightful shades from the night air. I had been only seven or eight days in one of them, when the depot was removed into a convent near the market-place. This convent overlooked the sea, and commanded the harbour, the Spaniards having four pieces of cannon planted in the yard for that purpose.

We had two parades, and three guards to supply, every day: one guard over the wooden houses, one in the depot, and one in a distant part of the town. Divine service was performed regularly every Sunday by a clergyman of the establishment, who preached some excellent sermons.

St. Andero is a good-looking town, situated on an arm of the sea: it has a large bay, that will accommodate a great number of light vessels; and a good market tolerably well supplied with provisions. There are several convents and churches, and a number of curious fountains of water, I do not know the population, but I suppose there are six or seven thousand inhabitants. The greatest markets are on Sundays and saint days: on the latter days, cannons are fired, and great military rejoicings take place in honour of their saints, just in the same way as we fire and rejoice on the birthday of our king.

The people in this part of Spain are very bigoted, and fond of priestly show. I saw, during my stay here, several funerals, at one of which were carried about a dozen ponderous wax candles, each of them was as thick as a man's arm, and all lighted. One morning I witnessed an affecting scene with a regiment of Spaniards, who were going to assist in the taking of St. Antonia, a strong fortification at no very great distance from this place. The wives and friends of the Spanish soldiers took leave of them in an affectionate manner, praying earnestly for their preservation and success. This put me in mind of the embarkation of our regiment for Walcheren in 1809, when we left all the women behind, one excepted.

In consequence of a delay in the arrival of my accounts, as I have intimated before, I had to remain much longer at St. Andero than I otherwise should have done. Being invalided on the 20th of October 1813, I was in constant expectation of leaving this place for England. There were about one hundred men, whose accounts could not be settled; so that we waited one week after another, most of us being in want of necessaries and money. At this period, I had ten pounds due from the regiment. At length an order arrived from Lord Wellington, that all the invalids were to be embarked and sent to England without delay: a transport was fitted up in the best possible manner, and on Wednesday the 30th of March 1814, we were put on board. The vessel was very much crowded, having on board about two hundred men, several of whom were so exceedingly ill of their wounds, that it was with difficulty they were embarked.

On Saturday the 2nd of April the anchor was weighed, and we left Spain, the country in which we had endured so much and so long. On leaving it, there were no tears shed, unless they were tears of joy. For my own part, I was filled with gratitude, that Divine Providence had so far acceded to my wishes, and had thus preserved me from death in its most terrific forms. I could not help rejoicing that I was once more on my way to the best of nations. When I thought of landing in England, my heart fluttered with a sort of joy, which, cannot be described. With what great pleasure did I walk the decks of the vessel, my mind being occupied with the thoughts of home, and all its delights.

We sailed sweetly along the Bay of Biscay: the weather was serene, the sky clear; in short, everything seemed to favour our voyage to the delightful atmosphere of religion and liberty! There were several vessels in our fleet under convoy. A woman was on board our ship, whose husband was in one of the other vessels, which lay-to in order to take her on board. The woman descended into the boat, and was rowed over the mighty swells of the Bay of Biscay to her husband's vessel. I don't know indeed that there was any particular danger in this, but it was terrifying to see a little boat tossed on the mighty surges of this bay. On the 6th one of our poor comrades died, and was buried in the sea. On the 7th we got sight of the Land's End, and on the afternoon of Friday the 8th of April we dropped anchor in the harbour of Plymouth-Dock. The anchor had no sooner gone, than we gave three times three cheers, and almost rendered the air with our shouts of joy. Next morning, we disembarked, and marched into Racket-Court Barracks, after an absence from England of almost three years.

CHAPTER 18

Peace Proclaimed

On Sunday morning we paraded for divine service in the large barrack square of this place. A militiaman joined me and a comrade who was with me, and began to talk to us for our good. "I suppose," said he, "you have just come from Spain, and are both wounded?"

"Yes," was the answer.

"Oh," said he, "how good has the Almighty been to you. In allowing you to return to your native land! Thousands of your comrades have fallen, and are in eternity. God has spared you, in order that you may repent and believe the gospel, and be saved."

I really was ashamed, and hung down my head, for there were several people standing by at the time; but notwithstanding all this, I felt the force of the good man's reasoning, and respected him for his kind instruction and advice. We withdrew to our quarters, and, as it is customary in barracks to go early to bed, I retired to rest about half-past eight o'clock, feeling grateful to Divine Providence that I had been preserved in so many dangers.

On Monday morning I wrote to acquaint my friends that I had arrived in England, and was destitute of money and clothing, and that I was in a very distressed state. On the 13th we passed a board of surgeons, who would have invalided me for Chelsea; but having nearly completed my term of service, I requested to be sent to my regimental depot, which was granted. On the 14th, all the men that were ordered for their respective regimental depots were sent to St. Nicholas, or Drake's Isle, in Plymouth Sound, on this island twenty-eight pieces of cannon were mounted.

The only persons here were the storekeeper, a free man of Great Grimsby, and an old woman who kept the canteen or public-house, and sold bread and groceries to the soldiers in the barracks. The whole extent of the island, is not more than two or three acres. St. Nicholas

Island commands the Sound and entrances to Plymouth and Plymouth-Dock harbours. To the west stands the elegant mansion of the Earl of Mount-Edgcumbe. His Lordship has a battery of several pieces of cannon in front of his seat, which is delightfully situated. We were about two miles from Dock, and nearly one and a half from Stonehouse, from whence we received our provisions three times a week. Our detachment was under the command of Captain Maxwell, of the Royal Monaghan Militia, which was then stationed at Dock.

On the 28th, an answer to my letter arrived, containing a one-pound note, which was indeed acceptable. The promptitude with which my letter was answered, proved that, notwithstanding my long absence from home, my friends had not forgotten to sympathize with me in my forlorn condition. While we were here, peace was proclaimed, and in honour of it, the dock-yard people had one of the grandest processions ever known at Plymouth-Dock: the town was illuminated in every part, and transparencies were exhibited in the windows. I obtained liberty of the captain to go and view the illumination.

In a few days several French ships of war arrived, loaded with prisoners, and took several hundreds of their own men back with them to France. It was truly delightful to see a mutual exchange of men. With what light hearts did the poor French prisoners embark on board the vessels of their own country! Some of them had been in England ten or twelve years. I saw hundreds of them embarked at different periods. One circumstance, when they were embarking, took my attention very much, and that was the distribution of Testaments and religious books by the agents of the British and Foreign Bible Society.

On one occasion I witnessed the embarkation of about four hundred: previous thereto, three or four porters arrived, loaded with boxes, which they laid on the beach: presently two gentlemen came and opened them: they were full of Bibles, Testaments, and other religious books, in the French language. The prisoners arrived, and the gentlemen then commenced their labour of Christian charity and love, by distributing to every man, as he stepped into the boat a Bible, Testament, or Religious Tract. Some of the Frenchmen received them with a cold indifference, while others testified their approbation by thankfully receiving the books, and pronouncing many blessings on the giver, and on the British Nation for their generosity.

I must not omit to relate an affair which occurred on our island. Certain officers, who were acquainted with the captain, had begun to smuggle, and to carry on a considerable traffic in contraband goods. They had contrived to get a large quantity of brandy, hollands, and wine, from, a French ship of war, which lay in the Sound, and had lodged them among the military stores of this place. The next morning, I mounted guard. We had learnt their proceeding, and formed a plan to make the colonel who was the leading man, give us a good treat, or not let him remove the liquors from the stores.

Night coming on, the colonel arrived with his pleasure-boat, on a pretended visit to the captain: about ten the colonel opened the stores, and began to remove the brandy, little thinking that we had been let into the secret. The corporal had given strict orders to the sentinel how to act. When the colonel came to the strong garrison doors, which were double, he ordered the sentinel to open them. "No," said he, "that is against my orders."

The colonel then began to open them himself, and to force past, and would have accomplished his purpose, had it not been for myself and another of the guard, who interfered, saying, "No, no, sir; you must not force the sentry."

"Do you know who I am?" said the colonel.

"Yes, very well, but you will not frighten us; and one might have thought that you, a colonel of a regiment, should have known better than to have attempted to force a sentinel: the commanding officer of this place dare not act in this way."

The colonel then became calm, and promised to give us a guinea, if we would allow him to pass the guard. We consented: the hampers were removed to the beach, and some of them put into the boat. When, suddenly the custom-house boat ran on the beach! The officer jumped out and seized the colonel's boat and liquors: the guard immediately shut the doors, and challenged them. I stood upon the ramparts, threatening to fire upon them if they did not move off; but I had only a stick in my hand.

In the meantime, the officers in strong terms demanded an entrance in the name of His Majesty. During this period the men were running to different parts of the island to hide the liquors for themselves: two or three cases of liquors were thrown down the steep precipices of the rocks, and dashed to pieces. At length the doors were opened, the officers entered, and searched the place, but found nothing more. They then returned to the beach, and took possession of the colonel's boat. The colonel then, finding resistance useless, accompanied the officers, who pulled off from the shore with the colonel and his valuable cargo.

After they were gone, we divided the spoil that was left; but in the hurry and confusion, several of the bottles were broken. I got for my share three bottles of brandy. The colonel lost his liquor and his boat, worth fifty pounds, beside being fined three hundred; so that in all it cost him nearly five hundred pounds for his foolishness.

In the latter end of June, the detachment left St. Nicholas Island, and marched to Maker Heights in Cornwall. Our barracks were only half a mile from Kingsand, in the bay of which is good anchorage for the largest ships in our navy. At the time of our arrivals there were six first-rate ships of war lying at anchor. Near this place is one of the most extensive breweries in the kingdom: the navy is supplied from it. I visited several curiosities near this place: one was a telegraph on the top of a church.

On the 7th of July we received a route to join our respective depots. There were about two hundred of us, belonging to different regiments, placed under the command of a lieutenant, who had directions to leave the men at their respective depots as they arrived at them. On the morning of the 8th, we repaired to the ferry, and were taken over to Plymouth-Dock, and, from thence to Stonehouse, and there waited in front of the pay-master's house for the settlement of our accounts; after which we marched off to Ivy Bridge.

9th. Arrived at Ashburton.

10th. Being Sunday, we halted. Ashburton at this time was crowded with American officers, who were prisoners of war.

11th. We moved off for Chudleigh, distant ten miles, where I was quartered at the head inn; but the landlord lodged us with a widow, at whose house a most awful tragedy had taken place. In the latter end of May, and about six weeks from this period, a young woman, who had lodged in this house, and worked in one of the factories, had murdered her newborn child. She was a stranger in Chudleigh, and had concealed the child in a dunghill; but the following night there was a great storm of thunder and rain, so that the water had washed away the manure, and left the child exposed to view.

Suspicion immediately fell on this young woman, who was examined by the surgeons of the place, and it was clearly proved that she was the mother. A coroner's jury brought in a verdict of wilful murder against the unfortunate girl, who, after recovering, was committed to Exeter gaol; but what became of her I never heard. The reason I mention this incident is, that I and my comrade had to sleep in the room

176

where this tragedy took place.

12th. We arrived at Exeter, and after partaking of refreshment at our quarters, I visited the cathedral, which is very handsome. The great bell is a curiosity: it is much larger than "Great Tom" at Lincoln, but not so thick. I noted down in my pocket-book an inscription in the tower, which is as follows:

> This bell weighs 12500lbs., and is 500lbs. heavier than the boasted 'Great Tom' at Lincoln.

13th. We marched to Honiton, and on the 14th reached Axminster, where there was great rejoicing on account of the peace. On a green near the town a number of booths were erected, where ale and liquors were sold. In the afternoon the volunteers assembled, and having an effigy of Buonaparte placed in a cart, they fired, and some of than thrust their bayonets through the effigy. After this the officers dined, with several gentlemen in one of the large booths, in honour of the event. This was the best manner of fighting, for the victory was obtained without loss of blood, or the disastrous fatigues of actual service.

15th. We arrived at Bridport, and, after a fatiguing march, on the 27th reached Lewes, in Sussex, the place where we were stationed when we received our route for Spain and Portugal, it being three years and nearly, two months since that period. When I passed the barracks, I thought of the comfortable and happy moments I had spent in them while in the service of Major Thompson; and I could not help reflecting on the many vicissitudes I had passed through since 1811, at which time the 68th Regiment was nearly nine hundred strong—now dwindled into a mere skeleton.

28th. We reached Eastbourne, and on the 29th Ashford, where we found our regimental depot under the command of Captain Reed, who had commanded the company to which I belonged during the Spanish campaigns. He was pleased to see me again, for I had been his servant twice during our residence in the Peninsula. Here we received our new clothing, which had been due since December 1812, and whatever necessaries that were needed to make us comfortable. I was not required to do any duty whatever, having only to parade in the rear of the depot to answer to my name twice a day. At this period the depot consisted of nearly one hundred men.

In the beginning of September, Sergeant Currie, myself, and another, obtained furloughs to visit our relations. We left Ashford at nine o'clock at night, and reached Maidstone early the next morning; here we rested several hours, and then started for Gravesend, where we arrived in the evening, but had only just time to refresh ourselves before the packets were ready to sail for London. We sailed all night, and at daylight were, highly gratified by the scenery on the banks of the Thames. When we came, near London, I was astonished at the number of vessels on the river. I had never sailed up the Thames before, therefore I was struck with the grandeur and magnificence that appeared on every side.

About six o'clock we landed near the Tower, repaired to the Borough, and applied at the chief constable's for billets. I was quartered near the Bell, Holborn Hill. After refreshing ourselves, we went to our regimental agents. Greenwood, Cox, & Co., Craig's Court, Charing Cross, and there received our clothing money for 1813, and prize money for the Island of Walcheren. I was now richer than I had been for years; and my time was occupied for nearly three days in visiting different parts of the metropolis. On the 8th I took my departure in the Boston coach, and the next day arrived at Boston, after a very pleasant journey.

On the 10th I took my passage in one of the Lincoln packets for Dogdike, and that evening entered with a light heart the village of Coningsby. Mr. Cuthbert and family received me with a hearty welcome, and testified their kindness by making me as comfortable as possible. I spent a few happy days with them, and then repaired to Louth. Surely none could be more happy than myself. I had been from home almost five years, and nearly three of them in Spain and Portugal, suffering privations unknown at home: sometimes advancing in pursuit of the enemy, at others my constitution nearly destroyed by fevers; destitute of most of the comforts of life, frequently famishing for the want of provisions, and often compelled to lie out of doors without either tent or covering: this was particularly the case in the campaign of 1812.

But now I was near the place where sorrows of this sort seldom come, and where the demon of war is only heard at a distance. As soon as I got into the town, I repaired to my grandmother, Widow Cuthbert's, and found the good old woman still active and healthy for her years, being eighty-five. Refreshment was brought, and I partook of a meal under the roof of her whom I never expected to see again. Amongst my numerous relations and friends, none were more solicitous, for my welfare than my old master and mistress Foggitt: these kind friends were always glad to see me. The time of my leave of absence was spent amongst my friends in a very pleasant and delightful manner: I related to them the many things that had been witnessed and endured by me, and I really found it far more comfortable to relate these facts without being subject to the continual fatigues and dangers of war.

After remaining at Louth as long as my furlough would admit, I repaired to Coningsby, where I remained about three days. I then went to Boston, and took the coach for London, and arrived thither on Sunday the 9th of October: there I learned that the regimental depot had marched for Ireland. Captain M'Kay being at an inn at Charing Cross, I repaired thither, to enquire of him: he informed me that they were at Chichester, waiting for a transport to take them to Ireland, and that it would be a week or more before they sailed. He also told me that my old master, Major Thompson, was in London. On Monday morning, after a walk of four miles, I arrived at his lodgings: as soon as he saw me, he took me by the hand, saying, he was glad to see me again. After talking with me on different subjects, he gave me a pressing invitation to call at his house at Okenham, Berkshire, when I returned from Ireland. At parting he gave me a very handsome present in cash, again requesting me to call upon him when I returned.

On Wednesday the 12th I left London, and on the following evening joined the depot at Chichester. On the 18th we marched to Hilsea barracks, and were there quartered for the evening. On the following morning we marched to Portsmouth, and embarked on board a transport, together with our heavy baggage. On the 21st, several men and women of different regiments were put on boards making our number amount to about two hundred soldiers, thirty women, and as many children, so that we were uncommonly crowded.

CHAPTER 19

Is Discharged

About the 29th the anchor was weighed, and we set sail for Ireland, and after a pleasant voyage of three days reached the Cove of Cork, where we disembarked about seventy men and women, whose regiments were in this part of Ireland. Our vessel lay at Cove about seven days, and we received large supplies of vegetables to our salt provisions, which made our situation more comfortable. On the afternoon of the 10th, the anchor was again weighed, and we sailed for Carlingford, in the north of Ireland. Our voyage was pleasant until midnight, when it began to blow very fresh, and there was a considerable swell on the ocean, but towards morning there was a complete storm, the sea ran mountains high, the rain fell in torrents, and everything had a most terrific appearance: the storm continued during the whole day, and the sea was awfully agitated.

Several heavy seas broke in upon our forecastle, the yard-arms of the vessel frequently touched the water, and nothing could exceed the dismal appearance of the elements. Above, the clouds were flying in constant succession, carried by furious winds; below, was the awfully agitated main rolling in mighty billows along. At one time our ship seemed elevated to the skies, at another engulphed in the vast abyss. This was our situation during forty-eight long and tedious hours, expecting every moment that the ship would be lost, especially as we were in one of the most dangerous channels in this part of the world.

After having passed through the fatigues and dangers of the Peninsular War, and on many occasions only just escaping with life—having been in eighteen or nineteen engagements, in which I was preserved in a very miraculous way; yet, after all it seemed as though I was to be lost on my passage to Ireland; indeed, few of us ever expected to see land. A circumstance occurred on the second night of this storm that made, some of us almost despair of being rescued, from our perilous situation. In the morning, a little boy, belonging to a woman of our regiment, told a person that his mother had got a baby during the night: it was thought a strange thing, as no one on board knew that she was with child; beside she had not seen her husband for three years and seven months.

Some of the women that were with us went to examine the truth of the boy's statement, and indeed it proved too true; for she had been delivered during the night, and had contrived to stifle the child. Her intentions, no doubt, were to throw the child into the sea, in order that it might never be known to her husband, especially as we were expecting to join the regiment at Belfast in a few days. When it got to be generally known amongst the soldiers and the people on board, there was such a burst of indignation from every part of the vessel, that some were actually preparing to throw her into the sea, saying, that it was she who had caused the storm. Others exclaimed, "It was a wonder that the Almighty did not send us to the bottom of the sea." I believe the captain himself did not know what to do with the poor wretched woman: in a few days, however, she died, and was buried in the deep.

The wind was still against us, being full west; the captain thought it prudent to steer for Cardigan Bay, South Wales, and about four o'clock in the afternoon of the 12th we let go our anchor, under cover of the land, and found ourselves once more in safety, and in a great measure freed from the fearful apprehensions of meeting a watery grave in these seas.

The wind continuing in the west, we sent our boats on shore every day for vegetables, but could not get half a supply. On the 22nd, the weather being more favourable, the captain thought he could get out of the bay: for this purpose he weighed anchor, and set sail; but before long we got amongst the breakers, and were forced to put about ship, and make for our old anchorage; During our short sail nearly all hands were sick, except myself, and it being beef and plum-pudding day, I expected having a good share: but the anchor had no sooner gone, and being in smooth water again, than their sickness left them, and every man was ready to eat his share.

On the morning of the 23rd, the wind being fair, we got on our way, and on Thursday evening the 24th of November entered Dublin Bay, and let go our anchor near the Pigeon-House. During the night a storm came on, and a vessel was lost not more than four hundred, yards from where we lay. The crew were saved, but the ship was dashed in pieces, and her cargo lost: in the morning pieces of the wreck were to be seen all along the sands.

On Saturday the 26th we landed at Dublin, after having been on board thirty-nine days, and part of the time on short allowance. We marched through the city of Dublin, and took up our quarters at a town called Swords.

Next day being Sunday, we halted. I observed that after the Roman Catholics had been to mass, a number of them collected at a public house near my lodging, and were dancing until after midnight. I understood it was a common practice amongst them. Nothing can exceed the miserable appearance of many of the public houses in Ireland, some of which cannot accommodate with a single bed: if you want one, you must apply at lodging-houses, of which there are a great number.

28th. We marched to a place called the Man of War; 29th, to Bilbrigan; 30th, to Drogheda; and on the 1st of December, to Dundalk. This evening I went to buy provisions, and found the people of this place great extortioners.

2nd. We reached Newry. I was distressed for the want of shoes, and in the evening repaired to the sergeant's lodgings for a pair of new ones. As I entered the door, two Irish peasants met me, and declared that I had knocked one of them down: the crowd collected about us, and had not some of my comrades come up at the time, I believe the consequences would have been very serious to me, for these villains were bent upon mischief.

On the 3rd we arrived at Hilsborough; next day being Sunday, we halted. I was quartered at the house of a poor peasant, who was compelled to labour for seven shillings a week the year round: he was apparently content and happy. On Monday the 5th we reached Lisburne, and on the 6th joined our regiment at Belfast. Having been absent from the regiment ever since the 31st of August 1813; I was exceedingly glad to see my old companions in arms again; but James Mann, my old comrade and faithful friend, who had so often been with me in distress and trouble in the Peninsula, was on furlough at Sunderland. The men had completely recovered from their late fatigues in France, Spain, and Portugal, indeed the appearance of the regiment was much better than could be expected; and after the depot joined them, they were nearly five hundred strong.

On the 8th I claimed my discharge: the adjutant, however, dissuaded me from it, saying, that if I remained until the half-yearly inspection, I should be recommended to the board. I asked the advice of Colonel Hawkins, who said, there was no need for me to remain any longer with the regiment. He immediately ordered the adjutant to make out my discharge, saying, he would sign it, and send me to Dublin to pass the board on the 28th instant. The colonel said he remembered my conduct on the 31st of August 1813, and would be as good as his promise, for recommending me to the board of general officers at the Royal Hospital, Kilmainham.

On the 10th my discharge was signed by the regimental surgeon, who described my wound, the ball still lodging in my body: it was then taken to the colonel, who wrote my character, then added his signature, which liberated me from serving in the 68th Durham Light Infantry. When I got hold of this document, I indeed felt what I had never done before: I found that I was a free man, and might go when and where I pleased without control. After receiving my arrears of pay, and subsist, and taking leave of my comrades, I repaired into the town, and took a private lodging.

On the 12th of December I left Belfast, and the 68th Regiment, and arriving at Hilsborough, took up my lodgings at my old quarters. My host was a Catholic, but accepted with thankfulness a Protestant spelling-book for his grandchildren.

13th. I left the peaceable abode of this old man, and arrived at Newry, a smart-looking town.

14th. I arrived at Dundalk, and the next morning took the coach for Dublin, and after a pleasant ride of about sixty English miles, reached it at seven o'clock in the evening.

On the 16th I reported myself to Messrs. Armit and Borough, our regimental agents, who took my discharge from me in order that my name might be entered on the list of those that were to pass the board on the 28th. I was quartered on a publican who would not take me in, but he gave me a shilling to pay for my lodgings, so that I had to wander from one part of Dublin to another before I could obtain lodgings that suited me. Being a very stormy day, several houses were unroofed, chimneys blown down, and in one instance a house was levelled with the ground: tiles, slates, and bricks flew about in all directions, and I narrowly escaped being killed.

At this period there were several soldiers in Dublin waiting to pass the board: we attended every other day to renew our billets. I frequently, walked three or four miles to my new quarters; but it was a general rule to give money to the soldier rather than be troubled with him, and I generally obtained as much as paid for my lodgings.

On the 20th of December a party of our regiment, commanded by Sergeant Harmon, arrived from Belfast, in order to pass the board: to this party H. Kenneville, of our company, belonged. Being a countryman of mine, and destitute of money, I took him to my lodgings, promising he should not want for anything until he passed the board. I visited several of the curiosities of this noble city: I also attended several places of public worship, both churches and dissenting chapels.

On the 28th, we were at the Royal Hospital, Kilmainham, by half-past nine o'clock; but the number to pass the board being so great, it was impossible to go through them all; so that the men belonging to high-numbered regiments were ordered to stop until the next boards which we expected would be on the 28th of January. Being amongst this number, I returned to my lodgings disappointed, and still left in suspense; but to our great joy we received orders to attend again on Saturday the 31st instant, on which day, about ten o'clock, the head surgeon began his examinations in the great hall. He closely inspected every case, and entered his opinion upon a list provided for that purpose.

When he had finished, he retired into the room where the board were assembling. After the commander in chief had taken his place, as the president, we fell into ranks, just as our names stood in the surgeon's list. The men now began to pass the board, and as they came out, each man was questioned as to what pension he had got. At length it came to my turn: the secretary read my name, the state of my wound, and character, aloud. One of the gentlemen said, "Nine-pence," another "One shilling;" but the majority were for nine-pence. I made a low bow and left the room. Kenneville, having no wound, nor much servitude, got only sixpence per day. We had orders to attend on Monday morning for our instructions, and half year's pension. We now returned to our lodgings, as delighted as though we had gained a comfortable independency, or had fallen heirs to some great estates.

The next day, being Sunday January the 1st 1815, I attended Divine service three times: if ever I felt grateful to the Divine Being for his care and goodness towards me, it was on this occasion. Monday the 2nd, we repaired to the hospital at Kilmainham, and received our instructions, and pension up to the 25th of June. We then went to our lodgings, packed up our knapsacks, and started for the Liverpool packet, which was to sail at three o'clock. Having to pass the Bank of Ireland, we changed our Irish for Bank of England notes. At length we arrived at the landing-place, and were taken in a boat to the packet; but such had been our hurry that we neglected to take a proper sea stock for the voyage: we suffered much by our neglect.

About four o'clock we commenced our voyage to England, and I never sailed before under such pleasant and delightful circumstances, being on my way home with a benefit of thirteen pounds thirteen shillings and nine-pence a year. Our voyage was pleasant for some time, and I remained on deck all night. The cabin being hot and crowded, I thought it better to remain above, than to be exposed to alternate heat and cold. On Tuesday morning the wind was contrary, being almost a head, so that we gave up all hopes of seeing Liverpool that day. The weather was not stormy, but we made little or no way, running first on one tack, then on the other, until Wednesday morning, when, wind was more favourable, and towards evening we got sight of land.

About seven o'clock at night we landed at Liverpool after being on board fifty-two hours with little or nothing to eat or drink, and being exposed to the open air the whole of the time, although it was a severe frost, and a great quantity of snow had fallen. When I stepped on the shore, it was with difficulty I walked to my lodgings, being so benumbed with cold, that I could scarcely get one foot before the other. After partaking of a hot supper, I anticipated a good night's rest, but I shook with cold during the whole of the night, and could sleep but little.

Next morning, I proposed to my comrades that we should walk to Warrington, as a day's walk would warm us. We left Liverpool, travelled cheerfully along the road, and were very social: no set of men could be more happy than we were. About two o'clock we reached Warrington, and took lodgings in the house of a shoemaker, who was careful to let us know that he was a Jacobin, by rolling in a most acrimonious manner against the king and government. This did not please either me or my comrades: we entered into argument with him, and told him at last in very plain terms, what he richly deserved. The poor son of Crispin was obliged to give up the point, or at least to be silent.

Friday the 6th we started for Manchester, walked about ten miles, then took the coach, and rode the rest of the way. We took up our quarters at the inn from which the Sheffield coach starts. Saturday morning early, we left by coach for Sheffield, where we arrived about one o'clock. After refreshing ourselves, we started for Rotherham, reached it by six in the evening, and took lodgings in a public-house, the landlady of which behaved as well as though we had been her relations. Monday, we reached Gainsborough, and from thence to a small village only eight miles from Lincoln. This being the last night we were together, we talked over a great deal of our late adventures in Holland, Spain, and Portugal, to the great entertainment of the company, who stayed until a late hour.

13th. This morning we made the best of our way to Lincoln, and arrived there about eleven o'clock. We partook of refreshment at the Adam and Eve public-house, where we parted: Kenneville went forward to his native village, and I that night lodged at a public-house near Bardney. On the 11th I started for Coningsby, arrived at the house of my uncle, Mr. Thomas Cuthbert, who with his family received me with gladness. I remained at Coningsby about three weeks, and then came forward to Louth, and found my grandmother and other relations much in the same way as I left them. All seemed pleased to see me again, and I was greatly delighted to have the unspeakable happiness to reside amongst them.

I was sorry to find that my old shop-mates were in the same state as I left them, having little more than half employment; so that there was no hope whatever that I could meet with an engagement, at least not until things took a turn. I lived with my friends until March, and then went to Lincoln, and engaged myself as a book-hawker. I returned to Louth, and on the following Monday commenced my new trade in the vicinity of Alford. My success was so indifferent, that I gave it up, and returned to Louth, being resolved to try some other way to obtain a livelihood.

I remained about three weeks, and then made up my mind once more to leave Louth, and to try my fortune elsewhere: for this purpose, I packed up my clothes, and sent them by the carrier to Coningsby, intending in a day or two to follow them. I by no means liked the idea of leaving home again; but such was my situation, that there was no alternative. On the evening of April, the 26th I bid my friends farewell, intending to set off early the next morning: I went to bed, cast down on account of my ill luck. About five o'clock in the morning, hearing a loud rapping at the door, I got up to know what was wanted: I was informed that my Aunt Green was dead, and that I was not to go to Coningsby.

After breakfast I met Mr. Adam Eve, who gave me employment at the carpet manufactory. After dinner I started for Coningsby, called at Horncastle, turned the direction of my bus, and sent it back to Louth. The face of things had now changed with me: having employment, and a little property at my disposal, I began to think of changing my way of life, and on the 1st of June 1815 I entered on the marriage state. In consequence of our trade being very uncertain, and subject to continual change, I fixed for myself in a small way of business, in which I have been the last six or seven years.

Thus far I have brought down the principal transactions of my life; and I now embrace the opportunity of expressing my gratitude to Divine Providence for the abundant mercies bestowed upon me. A soldier's life, is a very chequered one; and, as respects myself, the more I reflect, the more clearly, I perceive the goodness of the Almighty, and that I have been an object of his parental care and affection. While thousands have perished around me, my life has been spared; when I ill deserved it, amidst diseases, dangers, and death. May I ever be grateful for these blessings; and, having fought and bled in my country's cause, may I be found a true soldier of Christ, and be received by him as such in the day of his second appearing.

Conclusion

After the French were driven beyond the Bidassoa, on the day I was wounded, Lord Wellington made preparations for invading France. On the 7th October 1813, His Lordship forced the line of the Bidassoa, and by that means established himself with the French territory. On the 31st, the fortress of Pampeluna was given up into his hands; and His Lordship having now full freedom of action, proceeded to put into execution a bold and decisive plan of operations.

After considerable delay, occasioned by heavy rains, Lord Wellington, on the 10th November, attacked the enemy's positions near St. Jean de Luz, and St. Jean de Pied de Port, which he carried after a warm contest, taking fifty-one pieces of cannon, six tumbrils of ammunition, and fourteen hundred prisoners. The enemy then took a position in front of Bayonne, which had been entrenched with great care. This position was forced on the 8th December. On the 10th the enemy commenced the assailants, and made a desperate attack upon Sir Rowland Hill's corps, at Arcangues: they were, however, defeated, and lost five hundred prisoners, besides two whole regiments (Germans) that deserted. Another attempt was made by the enemy on the 12th, on the first division commanded by Major-General Howard, but without effect.

On the morning of the 13th, Marshal Soult pushed a large body of troops through Bayonne, and again attacked General Hill, with tremendous fury. The gallant general anticipated every movement, and drove the enemy back with great loss. They afterwards retreated through Bayonne, up the right bank of the Adour; and on the 18th the British Army was posted in winter quarters between that river and the Nive.

On the 21st February 1814, Lord Wellington opened the new campaign. After various skirmishes and encounters, a well-contested action was fought on the 27th at Orthies. The French entertained great hopes as to the issue of this battle, and they fought bravely, but to no purpose. They were driven from all their positions, and fled to Tarbes in the greatest confusion. Lord Wellington, having ordered Sir John Hope to sit down before Bayonne, and sent Marshal Beresford with ten thousand men to take possession of the important city of Bourdeaux, followed the French Army in close pursuit. Soult had retired into Thoulouse, and fortified it in the best manner possible. The Allied Army having arrived. Lord Wellington resolved to make an assault without delay. A long and severe contest ensued. The enemy were again worsted, losing sixteen hundred prisoners, and Lord Wellington entered Thoulouse at the head of his victorious army.

The Battle of Thoulouse was the last that was fought in the cause of the Peninsula. Buonaparte, as I mentioned in the introductory chapter, "left Madrid on the 22nd of January 1809, to attend to his affairs in Germany." Having brought these to a successful issue, he would have had an opportunity of bringing the whole of his overwhelming forces against the allies in the Peninsula, but, fortunately, the affairs of the north attracted his attention. A misunderstanding had taken place between him and the Emperor of Russia. An open rupture eventually took place, and Buonaparte set out in May 1812, with an army amounting to upwards of half a million of men, to subdue his opponents.

This was a fatal campaign to him—nearly the whole of his numerous and finely appointed army was destroyed by the rigours of the climate, or taken prisoners by the Russians, and himself obliged to return to Paris a miserable fugitive. Hither he was pursued by his adversaries, assisted by his auxiliaries, who had turned their arms against him. The combined armies entered Paris on the 31st of March, 1814. Buonaparte was dethroned and sent to Elba. A general peace followed, and the different armies returned home.

It was about this time that the Battle of Thoulouse was fought. The news of the general peace arrived at the headquarters of Marshal Soult on the 14th of April, and he transmitted the same to Lord Wellington. Hostilities now ceased, and His Lordship went to Paris. He afterwards came to England. His principal generals were rewarded with peerages, and he himself honoured with a dukedom.

Europe seemed now to enjoy the prospect of a lasting peace, when, in the early part of the ensuing year, while the allied sovereigns were assembled in congress at Vienna, Buonaparte suddenly escaped from the island of Elba, landed in France, hastened to Paris, and resumed the Imperial diadem, without firing a shot. His indignant opponents again came forward, fully determined to punish him whom they justly conceived to be the scourge and common disturber of Europe. The memorable and sanguinary Battle of Waterloo, fought on the 18th of June 1815, in which he and the Duke of Wellington met for the first time, gave a finishing stroke to his ambitious career. He surrendered himself into the hands of the English on the 13th of July, and was afterwards banished to the island of St. Helena, where he in a few years died a wretched outcast, neglected and forgotten.